Kudos for Travis Hearn's
Game Changer

My favorite moment in a sports competition is when the momentum shifts, and a team that seems destined to lose suddenly comes back to life and pulls off a win. It's always because there was a "game changer" that made the difference. You hold in your hands a book that will give you that same advantage in life! Through crazy stories of heartache and loss, Travis shows you how to change it up for an amazing victory!
> —Mark Batterson, *New York Times* bestselling author of *The Circle Maker* and Lead Pastor of National Community Church

Adversity builds character, and character builds greatness. Travis Hearn has a crazy story of growing up in adversity that could have defeated him, but instead, it transformed his life into one of influence and victory. Travis shares practical advice for keeping the right perspective on devastating losses and setbacks. You will be profoundly impacted by his street-smart, game-changing principles.
> —Miles McPherson, Pastor of The Rock Church

Travis Hearn has a story just like everybody else. What makes his story unique, though, are the incredible challenges he has encountered. Those challenges became a catalyst that propelled him into a position of great influence. If you are facing difficult struggles in your life, this book will inspire you and challenge you to take your next steps!
> —Tony Morgan, consultant, leadership coach, and author (TonyMorganLive.com)

What a powerful book! Game Changer will not comfort you. Neither will it confront you. But make no mistake—Travis Hearn will challenge you and the way you think about yourself, your role on planet earth, and your ability to be great and do great things. This is something ALL MEN both need and appreciate. Especially me.

—Kenny Luck, author of *Sleeping Giant* and founder of Every Man Ministries

As a pro basketball player, I've been a part of many thrilling game changing moments. But life is bigger than basketball, and at times, we're all desperate for a game changing moment. This book is infused with defining moments of hope that will inspire you to live your life in victory!

—Jared Dudley, NBA player with the Los Angeles Clippers

Game Changer is like a top 10 highlight reel of the most sensational and thrilling comeback plays in life! Stories that are courageous, contagious, conquering, catapulting, and captivating! Game Changer changes the game!

—Grant Hill, Seven-time NBA All-Star

This book will inject your soul with hope! It gives you the courage, the dare, and the audacity to keep praying and believing that your defining game changing moment is about to go down.

—Derwin L. Gray, Lead Pastor of Transformation Church and author of *Limitless Life: You Are More than Your Past When God Holds Your Future*

Having played in the NFL, I've witnessed first-hand just how fast the momentum of a football game can shift. Life is no different. Game Changer is an inspirational read laced with Bible stories and life stories that defy the odds and human logic.

> —Andre Wadsworth, Executive Pastor of Impact
> Church and former NFL player with the Arizona
> Cardinals

Mind. Blown. Those are the two words that I think of when reading Game Changer. It's absolutely incredible how God can turn the inconceivable into the conceivable. That's exactly what this book is about. God doing what God does—the impossible!

> —David Chrzan, Pastor and Chief of Staff of
> Saddleback Church

As an ex-Muslim raised in Pakistan who converted to Christianity and now a pastor in the United States, I know exactly what Travis means when he says Game Changer. God is a game changer! He did the impossible in my life and He can do the same for yours, too!

> —Naeem Fazal, Senior Pastor, Mosaic Church,
> author of Ex-*Muslim*

Game Changer is packed full of God-sized stories of how he turns grave situations into great situations! As you read through the chapters of this book, you will find yourself experiencing the exhilarating rush of God's hope even in the most hopeless of situations.

> —Danny Gokey, founder of Sophia's Heart, author
> of *Hope in Front of Me*, and national recording
> artist

TRAVIS HEARN

GAME CHANGER

The defining moment that takes
you from *trials to triumph*

NEW VANTAGE
B O O K S

I'd like to dedicate this book to God's greatest gift to me: to my wife, Natalie. Natty, you are the most amazing woman in the world. You are my anchor, my rock, my soulmate, my best friend, my game changer and my absolute everything. You are the most compassionate, kind, thoughtful, giving and selfless person alive. I love you. You are a game changer!

Acknowledgments

If any author ever had a critical list of people to thank "without whom this book would never have happened," I'm that author! I need to offer a few words to the phenomenal people who have been the game changers in my life and in this book project.

First and foremost: *Thank you to my wife, Natalie.* Natalie, you are a true Proverbs 31 virtuous woman. You're my dream girl, my soul mate, my best friend, and the most amazing woman in the world! You are a loving and selfless mommy and the most caring and compassionate woman I've ever been around. You are my foremost game changer. Since the day I met you, my life has never been the same. You have stood by me, believed in me, supported every lunatic idea I've ever had, and been patient with me. I love you.

Kylie, you are Daddy's angel and our very first miracle baby. Doctors said we may not be able to have kids, and within a year—boom—you came along! Game. Changed. You are an extraordinary, talented, and driven young lady, drop-dead gorgeous, and a ferocious basketball player—and all with a heart full of God. I love *you.*

Josiah, you were named after the eight-year-old king of Israel who "did what was right in the eyes of the LORD...not turning aside to the right or to the left" (2 Kings 2:22). And that is you. You're a game changer in the life of every person you come in contact with. You're kind, considerate, gentle, and a mighty man of God. Clearly, you are the next LeBron in the making. You are my one and only son, and I love you dearly.

Jazzlyn, you are Daddy's princess. Your very life is miraculous, and your personality is way bigger than your little four-year-old self. Daddy already has learned from you more game-changing principles than I can count. You are a sweet pea, Mommy's and Daddy's helper, the perfect little sissy, and always happy and joyous! *You* are the game changer for our entire family.

Mom, Chapter One says it all. You're the game-changer who's managed to walk in the light even during the darkest times of life. You are an overcomer, a woman full of God's Spirit and dedicated to Him like no other. Thank you for always putting me first and sacrificing your life for mine—a true model of what Jesus did for all of us. No wonder I love you!

Dad, you have become more than just a father. You're also an awesome friend, and your friendship means the world to me. Thank you for being a great listener, a loving man of God, and supportive in everything I do. I love you.

Andre, you are my best friend—a pillar in my life—and I can't imagine doing ministry without you. Together, we've witnessed God do the unimaginable through game-changing maneuvers over and over again. Thank you for backing me, loving me, and impacting Scottsdale with me. Scottsdale can attest: You are a game-changer!

Impact Church, my beyond-wonderful church family: You are truly sensational! I can't believe I get to be part of such an incredible congregation. You guys never cease to amaze me in your efforts to make an eternal impact. I'm honored to be your pastor and excited about the future. You are *all* game changers, and I'm proud of you!

Lee, you are a true friend. Through the years, we've seen God do the impossible time and time again, and it never gets old, does it? Thank you for being a game changer in my life, for believing in me, supporting me, and always treating me like family.

David Shepherd, the statement is so true that God is always on time. He put you in my life at the exact moment I needed you, and it changed the game! You're a genius—a professional and *exceptionally* good at what you do. Thank you for being my literary agent, my publisher, a man of God, and my personal friend. I look forward to many exciting years together.

Greg Webster, you are an editing phenom, a word wizard, and a sentence-maker *sensationale*. Talk about a game changer! Thank you for your tireless efforts in making sure *Game Changer* didn't come across like a first-grade book report. God has given you amazing talent and ability, and your work has made a major impact on my life.

And *Jesus*: You are my ultimate Game Changer. You took my mess and turned it into Your message. I will forever worship You. Thank You for seeing something in me that I didn't see in myself. Thank You for unconditional love, unmerited grace, and *eternal life*. I love You, God!

Table of Contents

Introduction

You are a game changer. You have all of the talents, gifts, experiences, skills, personality traits, DNA, guts, and determination to transform your situation, wherever you are.

As you read those words, *if* you feel yourself rising up to argue with me, thinking, "No, I'm sorry, but the *last* thing I would say about myself right now is, 'I'm a game changer'," then you need a serious overhaul of the way you look at yourself. You are meant to be a game changer in every sense of the word.

I've watched countless athletic competitions—and I'm sure you have too—in which a "game changing" moment shifted the momentum in favor of the team that had been struggling just minutes earlier. Sometimes the game changer wasn't a superstar athlete or even the best player on the team. It wasn't an intricate and creative plan laid out hours in advance by the head coach. In fact, the game changer was nothing you would have expected—which is exactly what makes the game changer so electrifying.

The *really* exciting games to watch are the ones in which the *least likely* player comes off the bench, walks onto the court or field, and blows everybody away with a game-changing play. How does that incredible moment unfold right in front of our eyes?

Deep within that unknown athlete, unseen by everyone around him or her, greatness was tucked away in the depths of that person's soul, just waiting for *the moment*. He had trained hard, learned more, prepared, disciplined himself, practiced the fundamentals over and over, and spent endless hours honing the game-changing potential within. And finally, in a stellar instant with everybody watching, the victory explodes. That's when people turn to each other and say, "Where did *she* come from? Where did we get *him*?"

Your Turn

More than anything else in life, I want that for *you*! In fact, I live for the moment it happens to you! Spurring you on to become the game changer God intends is why I wrote this book. You might not be a pro athlete who becomes the hero in front of millions on television. You might not be an athlete at all. Precisely what you do doesn't really matter at all. But one thing is clear: regardless of your current situation or background, you have the *seeds of greatness* planted within you to become a game changer!

Since the potential is there, it brings us to the question, will you be ready when the opportunity arises? Celebrated artist and World War II veteran Henry Hartman pointed the way to game-changing achievement: "Success always comes when preparation meets opportunity." That's what this book is all about—the *preparation*. Being ready for that moment.

You might think, "Well, Travis, that's easy for you to say. You're a pastor. You live in Scottsdale, Arizona, and you work with professional basketball and baseball players. What a charmed life. You probably grew up with a silver spoon in your mouth in a strong, stable, nurturing family." Well, not exactly; in fact, not even close.

Although I was certainly loved, I did not grow up in an ideal environment. My mom and dad divorced when I was just seven years old. The first few years of my life, I also lived in one of the worst neighborhoods in Phoenix. While I did pretty well in sports, there were probably a lot of people whispering behind my back about whether I was ever going to amount to anything. Correction: I *know* there were people saying that—and they weren't whispering.

I wasn't a church goer—unless you call "going to church" stopping by the church during a service, walking up the center isle to the front row while the pastor is preaching, leaning over and whispering in my mom's ear to ask for some spending money, and then walking right back out to go hang with the guys. Yeah. Totally rude. That was me.

So actually, the fact that you are holding this book in your hands is a miracle! That you have read even this much of my story should, all by itself, be incredibly motivating to you. If God can help me rise above my jacked up circumstances, my broken family, and my ludicrous early life, He can help you too! But make no mistake about it, those trying circumstances and those difficult situations were actually a *school of preparation* for me.

You have heard people say, "I went to the school of hard knocks," right? I am the poster child for that style of education. But I wouldn't trade my experiences for *anything*! In fact, if you're like me and you've got a bunch of junk in your past, then you should feel massive excitement about to explode out of your chest right now. You are about to find out that the crazy, horrific, disappointing, crushing, heart-breaking experiences of your life are *your greatest asset*!

I hope to accomplish two things by writing this book: to prepare you and to encourage you. I believe every day has a set of circumstances that *could* cause you to end your day in defeat. You know what I'm talking about. You drag yourself out of bed, hoping for the best. You get a running start on your day. You plan to get along wonderfully with everybody you meet. But then . . . *it starts*.

Somebody messes with you. Or the contract falls through. A meeting turns ugly. The phone brings devastating news. Your car won't start. And suddenly, you desperately need a game changer. I've written this book with those moments, and a million others like them, in mind.

Realizing Reality

I believe whatever reality we experience is based on our *perceptions* of reality. How we *perceive* the events and situations around us determines how successful we are at turning a situation around for the good. It all has to do with how we view the events and words, circumstances and dialogue that come our way. The key is to have the correct *filter* for the events around you. You and I have to consciously and constantly change the way we view life's events.

George Harrison of the Beatles once said, "It's all in the mind." Whether you like the Beatles' music or not (and to be honest, who doesn't love at least one of the Beatles' iconic songs?), Harrison was onto something: it *is* all in our minds.

We have to change the way we think, in order to change the game!

The Apostle Paul seems to agree with Harrison. In Romans 12:2, he says:

> Do not conform to the pattern of this world, but
> be transformed by the renewing of your mind.
> Then you will be able to test and approve what
> God's will is—his good, pleasing and perfect will.

Every single day, we have to do an overhaul of the way we think.

Hands down, the biggest change that turned my life around was the moment Jesus Christ got a hold of my heart. It was a radical transformation. I never looked back, and I was never the same.

I know many people talk about how they slowly investigated the claims of Jesus Christ and eventually made a *decision* to follow Him. It didn't work that way for me, though—maybe because I had so much wrong in my life. I knew I was racing down a street to nowhere, and I was getting there in an ugly way. So when I came to Jesus, I *needed* Him in my life. I was desperate for a solution that wouldn't let me down. Nothing but a complete change in the way I was looking at life would do! By following Jesus with everything I had to give, I discovered a radical power for my life. I'll tell you more about my crazy overhaul as we go along.

I'm not alone in experiencing this sort of transformed life, of course. Years ago, there was a group of guys who went through a radical change themselves when they encountered Jesus. They're known as *the twelve disciples*. Each one in this "dirty dozen" was just meandering through life, punching the time-clock, making a living, and then Jesus showed up and said, "Follow me." That's when absolutely everything got turned upside down for the rest of their lives! The purpose and course of their lives were forever altered.

I have organized this book around a set of twelve principles, based on the lives of these twelve biblical dudes. Each chapter is a custom-made shot of adrenaline that (I hope) is so entertaining and inspiring that you will read this book more than once, because you can't imagine starting your day without some words of encouragement and affirmation for your soul. I know I need 'em, and you do too!

Prep Time

Every successful athlete knows there are two forms of preparation for an intense competition: *mental* and *physical*. You might be totally ready to compete from a physical standpoint, but if you are not *mentally* prepared, you risk having a complete meltdown during a game. Mental preparation is where contests are won or lost. You beat your opponent in your mind first, before you ever walk onto the court or field. Just ask any professional athlete, and he or she will use phrases like, "get inside their head," or "beat them mentally."

It's hard for me to refer to Gregg Popovich, the legendary head coach of the San Antonio Spurs, without cringing at how much of a beast he has been at takin' it to the Phoenix Suns, time and time again. But I have to give Coach Pop credit for his incredible success with the Spurs. Many people try to figure out what has made him so consistent and unbeatable over the years, winning NBA championship after championship. At least part of his secret purportedly is what he calls "pounding the rock." He got the idea from a guy named Jacob Riis (1849-1914) who said this:

> When nothing seems to help, I go look at a stonecutter hammering away at his rock, perhaps a hundred times without as much as a crack showing in it. Yet at the hundred and first blow it will split in two, and I know it was not that blow that did it, but all that had gone before.

That is some fierce, focused, and determined mental preparation! You have to keep at it and never, never give up.

My two oldest kids, Kylie (13) and Josiah (10), are year round basketball players. They play club basketball for the Arizona Elite and the Impact Crusaders (*Crusaders*—what a fitting name for a pastor's kid's team, right?). My wife, Natalie, and I take the kids so we can be at every game they play. We are their biggest fans, and I love watching them play with all their hearts. Watching them reminds me of something I've said for a long time. It not only applies to basketball, but to everything in life as well: "The game isn't won with one amazing shot or move; it's won with a million shots or moves before it that prepared you for that moment."

Success doesn't just fall out of the sky and into your lap. Somebody who is immensely successful in any endeavor or business didn't just sit around dreaming about a cool way to make something happen or bring in some cash. They had to put a strategy into motion. It likely started with a pro forma to see if the income and expenses would balance out in a profitable way. Then they had to find out if there was a market for what they wanted to offer. They had to add staff and build or lease buildings to expand their efforts. They had to communicate their vision for the company with passion and clarity so every employee would consistently portray the same values and principles that were used to start the company. The list goes on and on. Their millions of "shots and moves" were taken behind the scenes for months, or maybe even years, before the "winning shot" took them to the top of their game.

If you want to be a game changer in every area of your life, I truly believe you must change *your* game—and change the way you think. When Jesus came on the scene and started His public ministry, He was a radical thinker, a change agent, troublemaker, a renegade, and yes, a *rebel*.

When the stuck-up church suits went looking for Him down at the big-T Temple, the religious leaders in the Temple hood sported a huge attitude about the young rebel rabbi: "No, bro's, the Nazarean dude's not here at the Temple. He's slummin' with the sinners on the street." Jesus really offended the Bible-thumpers of His day by hanging out and even *eating* with seedy people, the ultimate social blunder for a rabbi like Him.

Jesus gave us *game changer* principles to live by, and He passed them on to His posse of twelve guys. These game-changing *ideas* were hidden away in the Old Testament, written down by prophets and people who lived a long time before Jesus took on a human form. Jesus constantly quoted from these Old Testament principles, which did two things: (1) it made sure we didn't miss the timeless values given to us *prior* to the birth of Jesus; and (2) it gave further proof that the Old Testament isn't just a mythical story dreamed up by someone who wanted to put together a money-making, pyramid religious scheme. It was quite the opposite.

Jesus verified the truth of the Old Testament more than once, with clear references that immediately established the historical linkage to stories that have been dismissed by some as fairytales. For instance, I have friends who say, "Seriously. You actually believe that farfetched story about a guy named Jonah being swallowed by a whale?" Yes, I do! If Jesus believed it, then I believe it! And we know Jesus believed it because He stated it as fact, as recorded in Matthew:

> For as Jonah was three days and three nights in
> the belly of a huge fish, so the Son of Man will
> be three days and three nights in the heart of the
> earth. (Matthew 12:40)

Jesus also referenced the prophet Elijah and a widow who took care of him. He even went to great pains to illuminate the exact geographical spot where the miracle had taken place centuries earlier:

> I assure you that there were many widows in
> Israel in Elijah's time, when the sky was shut for
> three and a half years and there was a severe
> famine throughout the land. Yet Elijah was not
> sent to any of them, but to a widow in Zarephath
> in the region of Sidon. (Luke 4:25-26)

Jesus also throws some of His own game-changing concepts at us during His brief, championship career. In just three years,

Jesus picked up His title as the Savior of the world, not by coronation or a particular crowning event—not even by a vote, election, contest, or coup. No, Jesus claimed His title as Son of God by being executed in a gruesome form of capital punishment called *crucifixion*. He was sentenced to death in record time after an illegal, middle-of-the-night trial found Him guilty with no evidence. The prosecution hung its entire case on accusations from political-power-motivated false witnesses who were paid off by the religious elite, the Pharisees and Sadducees.

Why did they hate Jesus so much? Because He had true game-changing principles that made crowds of people want to listen to Him for hours and hours. The leaders were losing *their* influence to Jesus, the game changer!

The gospels are full of stories about hordes of people who were willing to sit on the grass on a hillside, straining to hear a life-changing teaching session from Jesus. He once had to stand in a boat on a lake while the crowd sat on the sloping shore, so the water's natural amplification could project His voice further into the crowd. The world has never seen—and never will see—a more powerful, relevant game-changing teacher than Jesus! I call Him the *Sermonator*. The Bible says people were "amazed" at His teaching because Jesus taught with great *authority*. I don't know about you, but I want to soak up all the teaching Jesus gave us, because every word of it is game-changing!

My goal here is to bring some of those game-changing principles alive in your mind. The only way that any of us change for the better is to believe and implement better principles. It's been said that the definition of insanity is doing the same thing over and over again but expecting a different result. We get locked into a pattern of "doing life" that gets us *nowhere* and desperately needs to change if we hope to get *somewhere* instead.

The reason for most of our problems is that something's been programmed into our minds at one time or another. For example, you might be full of fear because you were programmed to be full of fear by experiences you had as a child. Maybe you were physically abused or verbally assaulted as a kid. Maybe you were constantly afraid of being found out if you accidentally broke anything, even the silliest little knick-knack or worthless heirloom. Maybe you had to hide in a closet or stay outside while your mom and dad fought with each other, curse words flying, doors slamming. I don't know what caused it or how it happened, but you were *programmed* by those events to have an *automatic* reaction called *fear*. And fear can be fatal, but it doesn't have to be.

Jesus came to give you the *faith* and *courage* to rise above *all* of your fears. He was constantly telling people, "Fear not!" On more than one occasion, Jesus said, "Why are you so afraid? Do you have no faith?"

He wanted badly to impart to us this game-changing principle:

Fear will sabotage your life and keep you from being everything God has for your future.

In fact, the Bible tells us, "Perfect love casts out all fear" (1 John 4:18). Why? Because God wants us to know He loves us so much, He cares about us so infinitely, that we can rest in His complete and total love, knowing that He *always* has our best interest at heart.

When Joshua took over the leadership spot from Moses as he prepared to lead the Israelites into the Promised Land, God gave him these words:

> Have I not commanded you? Be strong and courageous. Do not be afraid; do not be discouraged, for the Lord your God will be with you wherever you go. (Joshua 1:9)

God communicated a serious game-changing attitude there! It's all tied up in the last word of the sentence: *go!*

Can you erase all your fears? Probably not. Will you ever be able to say you're fearless? I doubt it. But, as I tell people, "You can just start walkin'. You can move. You can go." One step at a time. No game is ever won unless somebody just keeps shootin'.

Another way to say this is YOLO (you only live once). Each of us needs to give it everything we've got! You only have one shot: this life. So jump into it like the championship game is on the line—because it is!

Do I have all the answers for every problem in life? Of course, I do (not)! But here's what I *do* have to offer you: I have a story of how radically Jesus has changed my life. I have a story that you can't argue with, because it happened to me, and I know I would probably be dead right now if God hadn't radically changed my heart.

I once heard somebody say, "You don't have to make *all* the mistakes in life yourself. Let somebody else make *some* of them." My prayer is that I made some mistakes *for* you! I hope some of my bad moves will make you laugh, make you think, make you get crazy-excited, maybe even make you cry. Most of all, I hope my mistakes, my story, my experiences, my ludicrous life adventures will inspire you and give you a radically new strategy for being a true game-changer!

Chapter 1

COURAGE

"But can't nobody (mess) with me. I'm like
toilet paper, Pampers®, and toothpaste.
I'm definitely proven to be effective."

—SHAQUILLE O'NEAL

Featured Disciple:
Matthew, the disciple who gave up everything to follow Jesus.

---

*"But Jesus immediately said to them:
'Take courage! It is I. Don't be afraid.'"*
Matthew 14:27

Courage is "the quality of mind or spirit that enables a
person to face difficulty, danger, pain, etc., without fear."
[www.thefreedictionary.com]

I'm just a normal dude.

Well, I suppose "normal" is relative. When people began encouraging me to write a book, I laughed and thought, *I'm pretty sure I don't have anything to write about that anyone would want to read. I'm just an average guy.* At that thought, however, I felt like God whispered to my mind: "What? *I'm* not worth writing about?" Ouch! Talk about feeling convicted.

I thought people were saying I should write about *me*, but whatever I have to write about is really *about God.* My bottom line is that I absolutely love Jesus. He's radically affected my life, and I pray He will inspire you through my life and this book. *He* is worth writing about *and* worth reading about.

Deep Background

I'd like to give you a little background about myself, but before I can give you *my* background, I need to tell you about my mama first. She is a one-of-a-kind woman with one of the craziest stories I know. Wait, no, *the* craziest story I know. Mom means the world to me, and she is the epitome of a game changer.

I admit that I'm a mama's boy, and she taught me more than I could ever say about life. She is an incredible woman of God, not because she was raised in a good home by super-Christian parents but because she was raised clinging to God for dear life. She depended on Him, not just because she wanted to but because she *had* to. My mom has never "had it all together," and she's been through more dark, scary, narrow valleys than most of us will ever have to walk through. She's endured scorching fires in her life and somehow, God has brought her through every single one of them refined like gold.

Mom was born in San Francisco, but grew up in Costa Mesa, California. She didn't know her daddy, and to this day, she's never met him and doesn't even know who he is (or, perhaps, was). She was as fatherless as they come. It's crazy enough that one-third of all kids today in America live *without* a father, but she knew nothing of her father. As if that wasn't bad enough, my grandmother was an unstable, alcoholic, verbally-abusive mother, and my mom felt a heavy responsibility for her two younger half sisters (same mother, different dads).

When my mom was fourteen, her mother was murdered and left dead in the streets of Chino, California. Can you imagine the devastation of finding out your mom has been murdered? This fourteen-year-old was left with no mother or father and the responsibility to care for two younger siblings.

She was a broken, scared little girl. Without a father or mother, she moved to a small town in Arizona to live with her grandmother—my great grandmother—to start a new life. What seemed like a dead end for her was really the beginning of something new.

I like to say, "A dead end is never *the* end,
but the *front* end of an opportunity to
blaze a new trail."

I've never fully understood why bad things happen to good people. My mom is "good people." She's also one of the most stable adults I know who has come from one of the most unstable and fractured childhoods I've ever heard of.

I probably shouldn't be surprised, though. The biblical writer, James, has something to say about how this works:

> Consider it pure joy, my brothers, whenever you
> face trials of many kinds, because you know that
> the testing of your faith develops perseverance.
> Perseverance must finish its work so that you
> may be mature and complete, not lacking
> anything."(James 1:1-4)

"Trials" are a tool, kind of like a knife. If you always use a kitchen knife to cut soft things, like a tomato, over time the blade will become dull and useless. However, if you scrape the knife against something hard, like a stone, it becomes sharp and ready to be used.

Although I don't know what you might be going through today, I encourage you to hang in there and consider it pure joy because God is making you complete. Your situation is no surprise to God. It didn't catch Him off-guard. Maybe you're facing hardships in your relationship(s), finances, health, or emotions; God knows exactly what you need and when you need it. He is always on time, and He wants to use your mess as a game-changing message to speak into your life. He can turn your trial into triumph and your test into a testimony.

Every test awaits a testimony,
and every trial awaits a triumph!

The Bible tells us about one of those great testimonies when we read about how the disciple Matthew was called to be a follower of Christ. Strolling through town one day, Jesus noticed Matthew manning his IRS booth, collecting taxes from people, and said to him, "Follow me." It's pretty amazing to read that Matthew jumped up and followed Jesus with no hesitation. Right then and there, he became one of Jesus' twelve apostles. It took some major courage to make such a huge change on a moment's notice!

Tax collectors in the days of Jesus were pretty much social outcasts. Good, religious Jews did not hang out with them because they were seen as a bunch of crooks. Tax collectors for the Roman government didn't get paid a salary. They were allowed to charge a "small percentage" of the taxes paid in order to make a living. Well, you can imagine how a system like that would work! How long do you think the "small percentage" would stay small? Probably about as long as it would take to set up the collection booth. Tax collectors took advantage of this windfall opportunity by charging much higher amounts to the people than just the taxes due. The Jews, who already hated the Romans who occupied their country in a hostile takeover, hated these tax collectors because they were agents of the Roman oppressors. They heaped double hatred on tax gougers, like Matthew, who were also Jews. These guys were *traitors*.

In the Gospels, these tax collectors—sometimes called publicans—are pretty much described by the society of their day as "scum of the earth." And all the while they are wheeling and dealing and making bank. They cut deals with people who couldn't pay their taxes and got a piece of the action on every single person who owed the government anything. They lived in abject luxury, so it was especially amazing that Matthew, when he met Jesus the first time, would have dropped everything, closed up his tax office, and followed Jesus.

You can imagine the company Matthew would be keeping, and he brought many of his social outcast friends and former business associates to meet Jesus, too. When Jesus accepted Matthew, the cheating tax swindler, His grace prompted the repentant scoundrel to bring boatloads of people to Jesus, who extended the same remarkable, un-politically correct love to them. Even though Matthew had signed onto a lifetime of hardship with Jesus, he had found unconditional love that made it all worthwhile!

Although my mom didn't start out in luxury like Matthew, she has been through a lifetime of hardships. As a result, Mom possesses insane levels of courage—Shaq-sized courage, to bring up my next sports feature.

Basketball maniac Shaquille O'Neal, as you probably know, is freakishly huge. Working with NBA types, I'm around tall people much of the time, but Shaq is beyond tall. Shaq is 7-feet-1-inch tall, weighs 325 pounds, and wears a size 23 shoe! He is larger than life in every way, full of personality, inspiration, greatness, *and courage*.

If you're like me, you can't help but smile when you read one of Shaq's quotable statements about his greatness, like the one at the opening of this chapter. While he was playing for the Phoenix Suns, his mammoth truck would be parked in the basement of the arena, with a not-so-subtle chrome Superman "S" emblazoned on the massive grill. It was totally fitting because you did truly feel like you were with Superman whenever you were in his presence.

For two years, Shaq attended chapel services I conducted as the Suns' team pastor. My favorite part of having him there was a ritual he followed with almost superstitious determination. When it came time for the team prayer, Shaq wanted to be right next to me. He stood so close that, when I would start to pray right before a game, he would place a massive hand on my head. It felt like his imposing "Shaqness" engulfed me. It was claustrophobic. With the palm of his hand squarely on the top of my head, his fingers reached down the front of my face, ending somewhere around my chin. The routine meant a lot to him (and did I mention, to me?), and it became an essential part of our pre-game routine.

Another measure of Shaq's size came up one day when he and I were having our picture taken together. As we stood side-by-side, the photographer couldn't get us both in the picture because I was so much smaller than he. But Shaq had a solution. He scooped me into his gargantuan arms and held me across his chest like a baby. The photographer didn't have to say "cheese." I couldn't stop smiling. As the basketball giant held me in the air, his arms began to shake a little, and I said, "Shaq, dawg, you're gonna have to start working those arms a little more, bro. You're getting a little soft!" He replied, "Nah man, my arms are just shaking because Trav got big ole buns!"

Shaq's personality, inspiration, greatness, and courage remind me of my mom. She may not be huge like the Shaq but her courage certainly is—freakishly huge, in fact, and her courage flows directly from her deep connection and faith in God.

Two years after Mom moved to Arizona, I was born. She was sixteen, and my dad was twenty. As crazy and traumatic as you and I might think this sounds, my mom was actually extremely happy and hopeful. For the first time in her life, she thought she could have a "normal" life. After all, doesn't "normal" consist of a husband, a wife, and a baby? For the first time ever, Mama could live the life *she'd* always dreamed of and give her *baby* the life she never had.

But their life together was very *real*. My parents got married, and the three of us lived in the hood. Fifteenth Avenue and Van Buren in Phoenix is no Mayberry, USA. Mom worked at a truck stop and Dad on an assembly line. By the time I was five, our house had been broken into several times, and any good stuff we had got jacked. Once, my favorite (and the only) watch my great grandfather gave me was stolen. I was devastated. It was probably worth only a buck, but to me, it was a memory from my great grandpa. No dollar amount could have replaced it. Besides that, there's nothing scarier to a little boy than having his house broken into, then surrounded by red and blue lights and hearing police officers shouting in the night. That's when my parents decided to move to a small town on the outskirts of greater Phoenix.

My parents were not even church goers, let alone Christians. I do remember, though, my mom reading from a picture Bible to me when I was about five. It told about the life, death, and resurrection of Jesus, and that book left a lasting imprint on my life. (Note to you parents: Try this at home—it may save your kids someday!)

By the time I was seven, my parents had divorced. Their separation wrecked my life. For weeks on end, I would cry and cry, asking my mommy and daddy why I couldn't live with both of them. I couldn't comprehend why we split up. It didn't make any sense to me at all. Unfortunately, Mom and Dad were just too young and immature to manage putting the pieces back together, so from then on, Dad became a visitor. Although I would have much rather that Dad lived in the house with Mom and me, I was at least thankful to have a dad in my life.

Several years later, Mom remarried, and a stepfather moved into *my* house. Awkward. Those of you who have lived through something like this know exactly what I'm talking about. From the time I was nine until I graduated high school at seventeen, Step-dad lived in our house. During those years, Mom and Stepfather had two girls, so now I had half-sisters. Then, when I was in high school, my mother fell crazy in love with Jesus Christ and began planting seeds of faith in my life.

About the same time, though, my stepfather fell in love with another woman. He left my mom, and, as nature would have it, he and this *other* woman had a baby, and so my sisters had another half-brother that wasn't related to me.

(Mom is on her third marriage now, but it's her *first* in which she is equally yoked. Both she and her husband are nuts about the Lord.)

Meanwhile, *my* dad got remarried and had four kids—three boys and a girl—with his new wife. So at this point in the story, if you're counting, I have three sisters and three brothers, four of whom are teenagers. And would you believe that early in his second marriage, both my dad and his wife got saved? It actually happened. After all this strangeness, my entire family, on both Mom's side and Dad's side, are Christians who love the Lord deeply.

So how about that for the "normal" life Mom longed for? It may sound like an off-the-chart dysfunctional mess, but you know what I say?

"Every family should create
and enjoy its *own* normal."

Somehow our dysfunctional mess now manages to function just fine.

The bizarre twists in my family story are a bit mind-bending, but if my mom had known her dad, and her mother had never been murdered, my mom would never have moved to Arizona. Which means I would never have been born, would never have been the chaplain for the Phoenix Suns, or the pastor of Impact Church in Scottsdale, Arizona, and you would certainly not be reading this book right now.

God's amazing ways are definitely not our ways. As the Bible says, " 'For my thoughts are not your thoughts, neither are your ways my ways,' declares the LORD" (Isaiah 55:8).

Who would have thought that, out of one woman's life of dysfunction, God would raise up a pastor and you would be reading his book? I guess God "would have thought." He is no respecter of persons (Acts 10:34) and loves each of us unconditionally.

My mom is a game changer. The courage she's possessed is what has defined her character.

What about you? What hardships, obstacles, challenges, dead ends, or fears are you facing right now? I encourage you to have my-mom-sized, Shaq-sized, freakishly huge courage! Because you, too, are meant to be a *game changer*.

Prayer for Courage

Dear Jesus,

Give me the courage to be a game changer! No matter what I face in life, no matter what I'm up against right now, help me to count it all joy. I know my strength and courage come from You! I know my ways are not Your ways, and You are no respecter of persons. I pray that You turn my trial into triumph and use my mess to become a game-changing message.

In Jesus name. Amen.

Scriptures to Reflect on

Matthew 14:27
James 1:1-4
Acts 10:34

Chapter 2

FAILURE

"I've missed more than nine thousand shots in my career. I've lost almost three hundred games. Twenty-six times, I've been trusted to take the game winning shot and missed. I've failed over and over and over again in my life. And that is why I succeed."

—Michael Jordan

Featured Disciple:
Peter, the disciple who came back from failure to achieve greatness.

"The godly may trip seven times, but they will get up again. But one disaster is enough to overthrow the wicked."
Proverbs 24:16 (NLT)

Failure is "the condition or fact of not achieving the desired end or result—being insufficient or falling short—a cessation of proper functioning or performance."
[www.thefreedictionary.com]

If you're like me and you've never failed at anything, you're welcome to skip over this chapter. On the other hand, if you picked up on the facetiousness of my statement and, like me and everyone else, you've endured your share of failure in life, read on. (Besides, what kind of author would I be if I really wanted you to skip over something I had written?)

One of the greatest enemies of courage is failure, or at least the fear of failure. I am convinced, though, that we look at failure all wrong. We think failure is a destination, the end of the road, a prediction of future trends, or an unshakable character trait, while nothing could be further from the truth. Until you and I conquer our fear of failure and the obsession to avoid it, we will never have the courage to move up to true greatness. Success actually *requires* failure. If Michael Jordan, the legendary NBA superstar, admits he failed in thousands of ways in order to succeed, then I am highly motivated to understand failure at a much deeper level. I've found that, the more you study successful people, the more you find that they failed constantly. So, how does this work? How does failure bring success?

A Failure of Biblical Proportions

Whether you are a believer in Jesus or not, you likely have heard the bizarre story about Peter and how he failed Jesus. Most people remember it, because it involves a farm animal—or at least they think it does. I'll share a fascinating bit of background about that "rooster," but first let me remind you of the story.

Just forty-eight hours before Jesus was about to be tortured and killed on a cross, He predicted right to Peter's face that Peter would deny Him, not just once, but *three* times, and Jesus even gave the timing of it. He said, "Before the rooster crows, you will deny me three times." Peter thought that was a ridiculous accusation, and he fired back at Jesus, "I would never deny you!" (You can see this one coming, can't you?)

Sure enough, after Jesus had been arrested and taken prisoner, Peter followed at a distance to see what would happen. Several people came up to Peter and said things like, "Hey, I recognize you! You're with that guy, Jesus!" But Peter denied knowing Jesus. A little time passed and then, these verses hit home:

> He [Peter] denied it again, with an oath: "I don't know the man!" After a little while, those standing there went up to Peter and said, "Surely you are one of them; your accent gives you away." Then he began to call down curses, and he swore to them, "I don't know the man!" (Matthew 26:72-74)

Oh, Peter! How could you? And right about then, the rooster Jesus had warned about crowed.

So now let me tell you about the *rooster* and what it meant to Peter. Many biblical scholars these days believe this was not referring to a farm bird. The rooster or cock crowing was a first century Jewish expression that referred to the "Temple crier." It's the person who called out or sounded a trumpet in the morning to summon priests to the Temple for the day's work and everyone else to prayer. It was a reminder to "put God first" every day, and what had Peter just done? He had put God *last*— *dead* last. He spurned the very One he had once called "the Messiah, the Son of the living God"!

After his third denial, Peter turned, saw Jesus look over at him from a distance, and the once-confident disciple was devastated. He had failed. He had failed Jesus. Big time!

Yet Peter's failure problems didn't start in that one, single night. They never do. All of us—and the struggles we have—don't happen overnight, do they? A really bad decision starts with one thousand smaller bad decisions along the way. If we're honest with ourselves, we know our issues have been building for a long time.

Peter was the same way. He was a liar who lived his life full of fear. When the heat was on, Peter was two-faced and disloyal if that's what it took to save his own skin. Evidently, he also had a problem with swearin' and cussin'. As you read the list of Peter's flaws, maybe you can even identify with some of them. And it might make you want to say to me, "Wait, Trav, the Bible says Jesus accepts me, just as I am, with all of my problems and issues and sin." To which I would respond:

"Yes, Jesus accepts you just the way you are!
But he is not content to leave you there!"

Peter, who experienced one of the most public failures of any disciple and whose shortcoming is documented for all time for all of us to read, also ended up preaching one of history's most brilliant and effective sermons after Jesus had risen from the dead. In fact, three thousand people committed their lives to Christ in response! This man who was a huge public failure became the greatest leader of the Christian movement, truly a *game changer* for Jesus Christ!

Failing into Success

One of my personal greatest stories of failure happened on the same day as one of my greatest successes. (Warning: this ranks up there with one of my mom's stories!) My high school varsity basketball coach, who coached me only during my senior year, told me the news one day that I had been chosen for the Arizona All-Star Team. I was *beyond* excited! I had dreamed of playing in the all-star game since I was a kid, and now it was finally going to happen.

My coach, who was in his forties, was so proud of me that he asked if I'd like to go out and celebrate with him. I wasn't exactly sure what he meant by "celebrate" so I asked, "What did you have in mind?"

My coach, unbelievably, said to me, "Let's have a few drinks to celebrate—and I'm buying!" Remember, I am all of seventeen-years-old at this point and not a Christian, so this sounds like the most amazing idea I've ever heard. Far from being cautious, I'm thinking, *Sweet! I don't have to find a buyer tonight!*

So coach and I roll over to a place with an in-home bar, and behind the wet bar is every kind of liquor known to man. I had never mixed a drink in my life, but here I had a hundred bottles of liquor to choose from. Although I'm clueless as to what to put together, I figure it can't be rocket science, right? So I start assembling my own concoctions—a little rum and some Coca-Cola into a glass, then another glass with a little more rum and a little less Coke, and then another with a lot more rum and not-so-much Coke. Suddenly, bam! I'm dizzy, the world's spinning, everything's a blur, and I still have to drive over an hour home. Scary.

Coach (I'm not sure how well his coaching judgment was working that night) and I jumped in our cars, and I headed out from the east valley back to my small town outside the city limits. I blew straight through red lights because my response time was so impaired. I swerved over every inch of road. Sometimes, I had all four tires heading toward oncoming traffic, and other times, all four tires danced along the shoulder. I am embarrassed and ashamed that I drove in such terrible condition that night. It is only by God's grace that I didn't hurt or kill somebody.

However, I can honestly say, it was also by the grace of God that . . . I got pulled over! I remember seeing red and blue lights flashing behind my car and thinking, *Are you kidding me? This just went from the best day of my life to the worst day of my life!*

As the police officer approached my car, I groaned when I realized he was an officer from my hometown. And this guy was not my biggest fan. He walked up and gloated into my window, "Well, look-ee here! If it isn't old Travis Hearn. This must be my lucky night!"

I got out of the car and proceeded to fail every sobriety test he gave me. I wondered who in the world had come up with so many ways to figure out someone had been drinking! *I'm so toast* kept going through my mind. I was obviously "toasted," but I just knew I was in for the serious kind of trouble.

The officer confirmed my worry by handcuffing me. He folded me into the back of his police cruiser and chauffeured me to the Peoria Police Department. Ask anyone else who's ever been arrested, and you can confirm the horrible, stomach-wrenching feelings I had at that moment. Being arrested is generally one of the worst low points in anybody's life. When you get arrested, your life shouts "FAILURE!"

At the station, the police asked me who had given me the liquor, and I decided, with all my seventeen-year-old wisdom, not to divulge that information, since the man who had done it was in a public position of responsibility, and he had a *lot* to lose. Fortunately for me, the police were not able to keep me in jail because I was a minor, so they called my mom. As I mentioned in Chapter 1, Mom was an amazing, godly woman, involved in her church, and on fire for God. I knew she would be disappointed in me. What I didn't know at the time was that, right before she drove an hour to pick me up from jail, she did something remarkable. Mom stopped by her church and prayed with a few people that *today would be the day I surrendered my life to the Lord.*

After she picked me up, we drove in silence back towards home. It was the longest drive of my life. I felt physically horrible and was crushed in spirit to know I had failed my mother so completely and upset her so badly.

Mom finally broke the silence: "Travis, would you like to go to my pastor's house?"

At first, I just ignored her, thinking that if I didn't answer, she wouldn't ask again. After all, it was approaching midnight on a Saturday night.

Mom waited a while, then persisted, "Travis, I asked you a question. Do you want to go over to my pastor's house right now?"

I thought she was crazy! I remember thinking, *No*, but I said, "Yes."

Quite frankly, I was scared to death because to me, this was like paying a visit to the Pope! After we pulled up outside the pastor's house, I dumped my can of chewing tobacco out of my pocket and into his front yard. After all, I was heading into the holy of holies. (As if my DUI arrest and trip home from jail was somehow not that big of a deal, but the chewing tobacco was! It's scary how the mind works—or doesn't—when you're wasted.) To show you how effective my dump-the-evidence plan was: when the sun came out, they found the can of chewing tobacco and knew it was mine! You see, the Bible even covers trying to hide chewing tobacco: "But everything exposed by the light becomes visible—and everything that is illuminated becomes a light" (Ephesians 5:13).

After dumping my chew in the yard, Mom and I walked up to the door and knocked. I was terrified, drunk, and embarrassed. But would you believe it? The pastor welcomed me with arms wide open! We sat down in his living room and began talking. Then my *real* situation hit me. Hard. I started crying, and I cried, and then cried some more. I needed *something* different in my life. Something real. Something new. I needed Jesus. So that night, February 20, 1993, I accepted Jesus Christ as my Lord and Savior. *That* changed my game!

The pastor, Mom, and I talked and talked and prayed and prayed. Mom and I didn't leave the house until 4:00 A.M. We stayed almost until time for church! When Mom and I went to church later that morning, I was *all in*.

My mom bought me a Bible, and I started reading and carrying it with me everywhere I went. I became addicted to the Word of God. Scripture was my new basketball. On Monday that week at school, my friends just about fell out, because I was holding a Bible in my hands instead of a basketball, and I was telling everyone I became a Christian. It was clear something had happened to me. The fact is, I was a new creation in Christ Jesus ("Therefore, if anyone is in Christ, the new creation has come: The old has gone, the new is here!"—2 Corinthians 5:17).

My greatest day of success turned into a huge personal failure, which led to the ultimate success of turning my life over to God. A great day had turned into a bad day which turned into the best day ever. What a roller coaster!

My story reminds me a lot of Abraham Lincoln's (kidding again, of course). Abe was da bomb.com, but he wasn't always perceived that way. Lincoln suffered through many failures and yet remains one of the most respected presidents in American history.

When he was only nine, Abe's mother died, an especially difficult hardship for a family struggling to scratch out a living on a nineteenth century farm. Lincoln ran for the state legislature in 1832 and lost in a field of thirteen candidates, even though there were four positions to be filled. The local sheriff seized most of his earthly possessions when his general store in New Salem, Illinois went bankrupt in 1834, and Lincoln took years to pay back his creditors. A year after the bankruptcy, Lincoln's sweetheart, Ann Rutledge, died unexpectedly, leaving Lincoln heartbroken and grieving.

In spite of these and other devastating setbacks, Abraham Lincoln was highly respected as a lawyer and a politician, and eventually was elected as president of the United States in 1860 and re-elected in 1864. Lincoln is credited with abolishing slavery in the United States and for preserving the Union during our brutal Civil War. Books, movies, documentaries, and numerous studies have been done about his life because he is a role model for . . . success.

The Failure Hall of Fame

What are your failures? Failure brings each of us to a crossroads. At the moment of failure, we have a radical decision to make: is this going to defeat me and define my life—or not? Failure brings up deep-seated questions that demand an answer. That's why failure is a game changer. Each of us must ask: Am I going to let this setback be the final blow, a knockout punch, the disqualifier, after which I will just watch from the sidelines, or will I get back in the arena? I hope you're tracking with me enough to scream the answer back at me: "No! This failure is not the end!"

Have you ever been thrown to the dirt in a failure of epic proportions—where all eyes are watching you fail? That was my scenario. The story of my arrest for DUI made the front page of our hometown newspaper. My headline: "Hearn Cited for DUI." How awesome is that?

The Bible gives us an example of a woman who went through a crazy, public failure scenario of her own. One day while Jesus was teaching, he was interrupted by a startling turn of events in front of a crowd:

> Then the scribes and Pharisees brought to Him
> a woman caught in adultery. And when they had
> set her in the midst, they said to Him, "Teacher,
> this woman was caught in adultery, in the very
> act. Now Moses, in the law, commanded us that
> such should be stoned. But what do You say?"
> This they said, testing Him, that they might have

something of which to accuse Him. But Jesus stooped down and wrote on the ground with His finger, as though He did not hear. So when they continued asking Him, He raised Himself up and said to them, "He who is without sin among you, let him throw a stone at her first." And again He stooped down and wrote on the ground. (John 8:3-8, NKJV)

Jesus' response to these guys was a stroke of genius. If He had said, "No, don't stone her," then He would be accused of contradicting Moses, which was a great way to wipe out His teaching ministry as a Jewish rabbi. But if Jesus had said, "Yes, stone her," then grace and forgiveness would have become just a nice idea from Jesus, but not something He put into action in the real world. Jesus' whole ministry was hanging in the balance.

Many people have tried to guess what Jesus wrote in the dust that day. Some have said He was just "doodling" while he waited. I don't think the Holy Spirit puts any words into the Bible carelessly, though, so I think the word "wrote" means just that. Jesus *wrote* something in the dirt, as in *words*! Maybe it had something to do with . . . failure. At the moment all these religious snobs were ready to pick up rocks to heave at this vile sinner, Jesus wrote something in the dirt with His finger.

Who knows? Maybe it was a list of failures—*their* failures. Specific failures. Greed. Lust. Envy. What *weren't* the woman's adversaries guilty of?

Let's face it. *Everyone* has failed at something. And any time we think we are justified in judging somebody else for his or her failures, we have ventured into the land of *selective memory*. We've forgotten the times that we ourselves have failed.

If you were one of the religious leaders in Jerusalem that day and you were about to stone a lady caught in the act of adultery, don't you think it would have rocked your world if Jesus wrote down one of *your* failures? The punch line of the story comes after everyone has left the scene:

> When the accusers heard this, they slipped away
> one by one, beginning with the oldest, until only
> Jesus was left in the middle of the crowd with
> the woman. Then Jesus stood up again and said
> to the woman, "Where are your accusers? Didn't
> even one of them condemn you?" "No, Lord," she
> said. And Jesus said, "Neither do I. Go and sin
> no more." (John 8:9-12, NLT)

Those words of Jesus should shoot adrenaline into your soul! They are possibly some of the most exciting words ever uttered by Jesus! This woman's guilt was undeniable. There were firsthand witnesses to her epic failure. She had totally blown it!

Her drama set the stage for Jesus to teach us how to look at failure. When He said, "Go and sin no more," He gave us the prescription for overcoming failure: look at failure as one more thing you *now* know does *not* work. Failure is the ultimate educator. *Failures become your list of things to avoid in the future, and that's how it guides you toward success.* Jesus forgives you! Go and sin no more!

Today, you might be haunted by your past failures. Maybe you are like me and have a failure in your life that is downright embarrassing to admit. Perhaps your failure is happening right now, or perhaps it's only been a few days or weeks since you failed. Whatever your scenario, you can feel like you're thrown into the dirt at the feet of Jesus, and everybody is ready to figuratively stone you to death. The world seems full of accusers and judges.

In your moment of failure, it is easy to get discouraged and depressed and to think your failure defines you. It's easy to believe the lie that failure is actually who you are. You're tempted to throw in the towel on the rest of your life and figure that you've ruined your dreams for the future. Enough of that thinking, and you eventually believe that you are indeed, *a failure*.

But that's not really you!

You are a game changer, not a failure. By failing at something, you've simply mastered one the concepts of what *not* to do again. As Thomas Edison said when trying to find a workable design for the light bulb: "I have not failed. I've just found ten thousand ways that won't work."

You are a game changer because you, with God's help, can turn failure into success!

Prayer about Failure

Dear Jesus,

Help me overcome my fears and move forward beyond my failures. Thank You for Your love, grace, and mercy. I certainly don't deserve it. I know my failures don't defeat me and don't define me and that I am a brand new creation in Christ Jesus. With Your help and blessing, I'm moving forward!

In Jesus Name. Amen.

Scriptures to Reflect on

Proverbs 24:16
Ephesians 5:13
2 Corinthians 5:17
John 8:3-12

Chapter 3

ACTION

"It's all about production, getting it done,
being efficient and doing it that way."

—ANDRE WADSWORTH (2007)
DEFENSIVE END, NEW YORK JETS

Featured Disciple:
Andrew, the disciple who brought people to Jesus.

---

*"So roll up your sleeves, put your mind in gear, be
totally ready to receive the gift that's coming when
Jesus arrives. Don't lazily slip back into those old
grooves of evil, doing just what you feel like doing.
You didn't know any better then; you do now. As
obedient children, let yourselves be pulled into a way
of life shaped by God's life, a life energetic and blazing
with holiness."*
1 Peter 1:13-16 (THE MESSAGE)

Action is "the fact or process of doing something, typically
to achieve an aim or a goal or a desired outcome."
[www.thefreedictionary.com]

I've loved to play sports since I was a little kid. When I was about five, I started playing T-ball. Then, as a third-grader, I did Pop Warner football, and I played basketball anywhere and any way I could. I just really, really loved sports. I spent all summer, every summer—no kidding, seven, eight, ten hours a day—playing basketball at the park. Sometimes I would even break into the high school gym (don't tell anybody that) just to play basketball because the weather was too hot outside.

I grew up with the same basic group of kids my whole life, too. We loved playing together and practicing together. During my junior year in high school, our team made its way to the state championship—big stuff for a puny place like my Arizona hometown. Our team was ranked number one the whole season. In fact, we were *undefeated*.

But we didn't just *end up* in the championship game. The state finals didn't just fall into our laps. Luck didn't get us there, either. Winning our way to the top took *lots* of hard work. And not from just one of us, from *all* of us. We worked hard individually, and we worked hard as a team. To be sure, we had a goal, a target—a *dream*—but it took *action* to get us there.

I learned as a scrappy young kid that it
takes lots of hard work and *action*
to achieve a goal.

It's not hard to set yourself apart from the rest of the pack; it's *very* hard! You have to work your tail off; you have to take *action.* Today, when I coach my kids, I tell them, "Go the extra mile. It's never crowded."

Action Figures

If there was ever a man of action in the Bible, it had to be Peter. But one disciple who doesn't get enough credit for his actions is Andrew. Even though Peter may get all the press for being a man of action, it was Andrew, his brother, who actually *brought* Peter to meet Jesus.

What if *Andrew* hadn't taken action? A whole bunch of stuff we now read about in the Bible would never have happened! When five thousand hungry people confronted Jesus on a hillside after a marathon church service, it was Andrew who scoped out the crowd and found the one person, a young boy, who at least had five loaves and two fishes to get the party started with. Then Jesus took over multiplying the food. But Andrew's action step is what set the miracle in motion.

Apparently, Andrew *and* brother Peter were the guys who continually *did* something. One night, when all twelve disciples were in the same boat, Jesus had decided to go for a stroll on the choppy waves of a storm-ravaged lake. But it was Peter who took action:

> "Lord, if it's you," Peter replied, "tell me to come to you on the water." "Come," he said. Then Peter got down out of the boat, walked on the water and came toward Jesus. (Matthew 14:28-29)

Peter is the only disciple who could put on his resume later, "Walked on water in the middle of a storm."

These two brothers never thought too long about anything, and I think there's something awesome about a person who doesn't get bogged down by the *paralysis of analysis* but who just plain gets after it! People of action are the ones God can really use.

Another time, Peter accompanied James and John up a mountain and saw Jesus in all His glory talking with two Old Testament dudes, Elijah and Moses (more evidence, by the way, that Old Testament stories happened just as written and are not fairy tales). Moved by the incredible sight of Moses and Elijah jawing with Jesus, Peter sprang into action with what I think was a really great suggestion:

> Peter said to Jesus, "Lord, it is good for us to be
> here. If you wish, I will put up three shelters—
> one for you, one for Moses and one for Elijah."
> (Matthew 17:4)

Peter was ready to whip up some condos on the mountaintop! And who could blame him? Any of us would have hated to see the moment end, too. So the man had the solution: build a resort on the slope. Let's hang here a while, bros!

The action brothers remind me about the story of the lone protester in communist China who made global news. Although we don't know a lot about him, one thing for sure is that he was a man of action!

In 1989, a protest swelled in size until it provoked the Chinese government to roll in tanks to calm things down.

Suddenly, out of the crowd, a solitary unarmed man in a white shirt walked directly in front of the column of tanks in Tiananmen Square, blocking their progress. Each time the lead tank tried to maneuver around him, he countered by stepping into its path. Watching on television, the world held its collective breath, waiting to see if he would survive the moment or be killed on the spot.

At last, a handful of people grabbed the man and pulled him back into the crowd, where he remained anonymous—and unpunished—for his act of bravery. *Time* magazine later counted the unknown rebel as one of the Most Influential People of the entire twentieth century. How cool is that?

No Fear Here

In his classic book, *The Power of Positive Thinking,* Norman Vincent Peale says about this action thing:

> Action is a great restorer and builder of
> confidence. Inaction is not only the result, but
> the cause, of fear. Perhaps the action you take
> will be successful; perhaps different action or
> adjustments will have to follow. But any action is
> better than no action at all.

Today, you might be tempted to shrink away from moving forward. There might be circumstances, dangers, rumors, worries, concerns, calculations, analysis, skeptics, publicity, obstacles, or a host of other reasons for you to stay put and not take action. But I'm praying that's not going to happen. Why?

Because, like I've said, *you* are a game changer, and game changers *do* action.

Instead of constantly convincing yourself why you shouldn't make a move, jump out there, and go for it! Picture yourself as Kobe Bryant or Michael Jordan, weaving your way down the court, unstoppable by any opponent, determined to make your goal. See yourself as Bethany Hamilton, who masterfully surfs the waves of Hawaii, even after losing an arm to a shark attack, and who now inspires thousands with her story of courage and hope.

Do this, and you will be known as a person of action. People will come from far and wide to spend time with you because they know *you* can get the job done. You will be respected by peers because you don't mess around. *You* get after it!

You are a game changer because you take action!

Prayer for Action

Dear Jesus,

Help me be a game changer who jumps into action! You know everything about me, Lord. You know when I procrastinate or put things off. You know how I can avoid moving forward. I need Your power in my life to make gigantic changes that will move me forward like never before. I really want to seize the day! I want to be a person who can be counted on to take action. Lord, please make this change in me.

In Jesus Name. Amen.

Scriptures to Reflect on

James 1:23-25
Colossians 3:23-24
John 12:20-22

Chapter 4

GRACE

"I have so many things to work on, and so many ways that I fail. But that's what grace is all about. I constantly wake up every morning trying to get better, trying to improve, trying to walk closer to God."

—TIM TEBOW

Featured Disciple:
James, the disciple who had to learn about grace.

"But he gives us more grace. That is why Scripture says: 'God opposes the proud but shows favor to the humble and oppressed.'"
James 4:6

Grace is "receiving goodwill and unmerited favor when the opposite is expected; Divine love and protection bestowed freely on people; the state of being protected or sanctified by the favor of God."
[www.thefreedictionary.com]

After I committed my life to the Lord, I found myself standing in awe regarding the grace of God. Even though I knew I had done some things that surely didn't please God, I started to really experience grace, the unmerited favor and love that God gives.

More than You Could Ask

One of the twelve disciples who had a particular need to learn about grace is James. This special need of his surfaces in Matthew 20, where we read about James' mom: "Then the mother of Zebedee's sons came to Jesus with her sons and, kneeling down, asked a favor of him" (Matthew 20:20).

From other passages in the Bible, we know that the mother of Zebedee's sons, James and John, was a lady named Salome. Most Bible scholars believe Salome was actually the sister of Mary, the mother of Jesus. Because Salome was Jesus' aunt, that makes James and John His cousins. So this was really a family matter in which "Aunt Salome" goes on to ask Jesus to give James and John the best seats in the throne room when He becomes King. She was all about getting top-billing for her boys, and they seem to have adopted the attitude for themselves.

The other thing you should know is that these cousins of Jesus were a couple of wild boys. They were the original "Dukes of Hazzard." How do I know? Jesus gave them a very revealing nickname in Mark 3:17: "James son of Zebedee and his brother John (to them he gave the name *Boanerges*, which means Sons of Thunder)."

"Sons of Thunder"! That sounds like me and some of my homeboys growing up—always making a scene, always kickin' up dust. These two boys were not wall-flowers. Jesus apparently had a couple of cousins who were pretty crazy dudes. In addition to whatever antics they were known for, they even had bad tempers. One time, when some people insulted Jesus, look at their solution: "When the disciples James and John saw this, they asked, 'Lord, do you want us to call fire down from heaven to destroy them?'" (Luke 9:54). Not exactly a "cute and cuddly" set of brothers. Cross these guys, and they'll pull out the ol' flame-thrower! James was far from understanding the message of grace Jesus brought to the world. (Upon hearing James' plan for total annihilation by fire, by the way, Jesus corrected him.)

I imagine Jesus was most likely explaining for the millionth time, "James, I'm not about revenge; I am about grace. I didn't come to rub it in; I came to rub it out."

I started out much like James, but instead of being punished, penalized, or sidelined for the sinful life I had lived, I found that God loves to pour out undeserved and unmerited blessings on me and people like me. Even with the many mistakes and sins that I've committed, I am continually blown away by the favor and grace God freely pours out on me.

There is no area of my life where God's grace is more apparent than with the details of how God led me to my amazing wife, Natalie. The way God brought her into my life is nothing short of a miracle, and the blessings since that day have been indescribable. God gave me the perfect soul mate. I'll tell you how it came about.

I started working as a worship leader in a medium-sized church in metro Phoenix. I was way in love with Jesus and poured my heart into serving Him. To say I was a Jesus Freak would be an understatement. Whenever I led worship, I would scan the congregation, hoping to spot any first-time guests, so I could talk to them afterwards, connect with them, and get them plugged into church.

During my audience scan one Sunday, my eyes riveted on a first-timer who was really caught up in worship, who happened to be my age, and who also happened to be *ravishingly beautiful*! I remember the scene like it was yesterday. We were singing "Amazing Grace" at that moment, but all I could think was, "Man, that's an Amazing Babe!"

As the weeks went by, I told God, "Lord, that girl—I want her for me! Can you make that happen?" Finally, I struck up a conversation with her after one service, and she really didn't seem to care. Okay, that's an understatement. She actually wanted nothing whatsoever to do with me! Of course, I decided that just meant she didn't grasp the amazing opportunity right in front of her eyes.

When your dreams for the future seem really
impossible and far away, that is when you
need to lean on God's grace and favor, and
watch how God will work it out for you.

I found out that she lived in Tucson, two hours away, where she attended the University of Arizona. Little by little, I also found out that she was a big-time career girl. She had helped a computer software company "go public" and was a marketing director, knockin' down big bucks, as opposed to me, who was knockin' down some relatively small bucks—miniscule, in fact, compared to her. Suddenly, it seemed really distant that she could ever be interested in me, so I decided just to lean on God's grace.

I discovered she had recently committed her life to Christ, like me, and was just as fired up as I was. She made the Sunday drive to Phoenix to the church where I was serving because her parents attended there. In my ongoing attempt to show myself as a great opportunity for her, I took advantage of an announcement one Sunday that our church would be feeding the homeless at a shelter downtown. It gave me the opening I needed to move our relationship (at least the one I had in mind) to the next level. I asked Natalie if she was interested in helping serve food at the shelter with me on Saturday. She shocked me by replying, "You know what? Maybe I will come do that."

I decided it was a *date*, and sure enough, we headed out the next Saturday to serve eggs and bacon together at the homeless shelter. In fact, we spent our first *three* dates serving food to homeless people and had a great time! After that, we went to the mall and hung out for a while. Of course, Natalie will tell you they were *not* dates, but those semantics don't matter. It got us started. In her mind, it was ministry, not romance, but I think ministry can be pretty romantic when you're serving God side by side!

In all seriousness, I believe serving the Lord *together* is one of the best ways for two people to start a God-centered relationship.

Twelve months after we started working together at the homeless shelter, we married and headed off for our life of whatever adventure God had for us. Natalie moved from Tucson to Phoenix to be in ministry and gave up her six-figure salary to take a job as a church receptionist for six bucks an hour. That showed me how much her heart was in ministry and how much she was committed to God's call on our lives. It was an amazingly exciting time in our life, thanks to God's grace!

Taxed by Grace

One of my favorite Bible stories centers on Jesus' interaction with a jerk from the Israeli IRS. His name was Zach. Zach was rich, but he made his living by cheating people. Yet the wild thing about Zach was that, even though he had everything, he felt like a great big nobody, and this deep, empty feeling brought him to a crisis about the time Jesus came along.

Zach had heard about someone named Jesus who could change his life, but it would take a miracle for cheatin' Zach to get an audience with this miracle-working teacher who was the talk of the town. Well, just like the miracle God worked for me to marry Natalie, God also worked a miracle for Zach to talk with Jesus. Here's how it happened:

> Jesus entered Jericho and was passing through.
> A man was there by the name of Zacchaeus; he
> was a chief tax collector and was wealthy. He
> wanted to see who Jesus was, but being a short
> man he could not, because of the crowd. So he
> ran ahead and climbed a sycamore-fig tree to
> see him, since Jesus was coming that way. When

Jesus reached the spot, he looked up and said to him, "Zacchaeus, come down immediately. I must stay at your house today." So he came down at once and welcomed him gladly. All the people saw this and began to mutter, "He has gone to be the guest of a 'sinner.'" But Zacchaeus stood up and said to the Lord, "Look, Lord! Here and now I give half of my possessions to the poor, and if I have cheated anybody out of anything, I will pay back four times the amount." Jesus said to him, "Today salvation has come to this house, because this man, too, is a son of Abraham. For the Son of Man came to seek and to save what was lost." (Luke 19:1-10)

In spite of all the foolish ways Zach had messed up his life, Jesus didn't even mention them. All He said was, "Z, I must stay at your house today."

With Jesus, relationship always trumps retribution.

The Lord always starts with grace and takes it from there.

You might be tempted to think you don't deserve anything good to happen in your life. Just like me assessing my chances with Natalie, you can't imagine that God would blow your mind with something so incredibly awesome. You might even try to sabotage yourself, giving in to negative thoughts that God is somehow disgusted with you and doesn't want to bless you.

If I were to say to some people that "God is getting ready to bless you with an extra load of grace," their first thought would be, "No, there is no way right now. I have a hard time believing that God is interested in pouring His grace out on me. Like Zach, I've done terrible stuff. I have some glaring limitations, struggles, and *issues*. I can't believe God would do a miracle for me."

That's what many people think when it comes to miracles. But . . . not you! Why? Do you know the answer yet? Sure you do: *You* are a game changer! Game changers live by God's grace.

If you let the grace of God sink into your heart and soul, you will start to realize that you can trust and rest in His provision and blessing for your life. Stress will slowly melt away. Why worry, when you know God is constantly watching out for your best interests and wants your life to go beyond your wildest dreams and hopes for the future? All your striving and figuring out a way for things to come together is hopelessly inadequate compared to resting in the almighty grace of God.

You are a game changer because you no longer try to make it happen on your own. You change the game by resting in the perfect grace of God!

Prayer for Grace

Dear Jesus,

I need Your grace in my life to really be a game changer. I can't possibly live up to the standard of being perfect and holy, so thank You for taking that load off my shoulders and for giving me a much lighter load, which is to just get to know You. Help me abide in You. Help me rest in Your grace. Teach me, Lord, how to be aware of Your grace every second of my day.

In Jesus Name. Amen.

Scriptures to Reflect on

Hebrews 4:16
2 Corinthians 12:8-9
Acts 6:8

Chapter 5

LEARNING

Whatever luck I had, I made. I was never a natural athlete, but I paid my dues in sweat and concentration and took the time necessary to learn karate and become world champion.

—CHUCK NORRIS

Featured Disciple:
Nathanael, the scoffer Jesus called to greater things.

"Let the wise listen and add to their learning, and let the discerning get guidance—for understanding proverbs and parables, the sayings and riddles of the wise. The fear of the Lord is the beginning of knowledge, but fools despise wisdom and instruction."
Proverbs 1:5-7

Learning is the act or experience of one that learns; knowledge or skill acquired by instruction or study; modification of a behavioral tendency by experience."
[www.thefreedictionary.com]

If you were to go back and talk to some of the mentors early in my life, I am sure they would tell you that I seemed to never *learn*. My senior pastor, Duane Middleton, in particular, reminded me often that I was slow to learn and *very* slow to pick up on subtle hints.

One time, for instance, I was helping get ready for a church service, but actually, I wasn't helping all that much. I was *really* just standing around, talking to anybody who would talk to me. I was a social butterfly and loved visiting with people, having fun, and joking around. What I failed to notice was that my senior pastor was *working*, as in *killin' it*, and there I was, not even noticing that I was jawin' away while he was doing all the work. He set up the chairs, the sound system, the tables, and everything else that goes into putting together a mobile church in a school gymnasium.

Finally, he walked by me and said, "You're gonna 'get it' one of these days."

I thought to myself, *Get what? I just got saved. I have Jesus. What else is there to get?*

So I asked him, "Pastor, get what? I'm gonna get what one of these days? What are you talking about?"

And he simply repeated himself, "Don't worry, you're gonna get it one of these days!"

I laugh to think about it now, and I imagine he will laugh too when he reads this book. He was *obviously* referring to my amazing ability to *not notice*, to be completely oblivious when there was a life lesson to be learned. I imagine he was thinking, *Surely Travis will notice that I am working my butt off, and he's cruisin' without a care in the world.* Sorry, pastor, that was a pretty naive assumption to make about me at that time in my life, but I have learned to learn—which is a key to any success-ful, game-changing life. Learn how to learn!

This same pastor used to tell me, "Travis, most things in life are caught, not taught." And, boy, was he sooo right. After a while, the lesson I was learning to learn dawned on me: I was actually supposed to *serve and help* with setting up the church and tearing it down. Imagine that! Me, actually *serving*. I was slow on the uptake but finally "got" this thing called servanthood.

Learning to Serve

When it comes to serving, not everything has to be given to you on a checklist. "See a need, fill a need" is the right approach. Duane never told me to help. I eventually (a very long overdue eventually) picked up on seeing a need and filling it by watching him. So the takeaway here is that my part and your part is to be *watching* to see what lessons might be right in front of our eyes but that we are in danger of missing. We have to view life as an opportunity for continual learning and improvement.

One of the disciples who had to learn to learn was Nathanael, or Bartholomew as he is called in some books of the New Testa-ment. Jesus first called Nathanael's friend Philip, and the Bible tells us that Philip immediately went and found Nathanael to tell him about Jesus:

> Philip found Nathanael and told him, "We have
> found the one Moses wrote about in the Law, and
> about whom the prophets also wrote—Jesus of
> Nazareth, the son of Joseph." (John 1:45)

Nathanael's reaction cracks me up, because I can imagine somebody saying the same thing about me: " 'Nazareth! Can anything good come from there?' Nathanael asked" (John 1:46).

"What? That po-dunk town of Wickenburg? Can anything good come from there?" Trust me, it's been said of me.

Philip wasn't put off by Nathanael's jeering. In fact, he had just the right answer for him: "Come and see." He might as well have said, "Come and *learn*!"

The fun part of this scene is that the story gets better. Nathanael was about to get a dose of old school schoolin' straight from Jesus. Jesus knew a scoffer and a smart-butt when He saw one, and He saw Nathanael coming a mile away: "When Jesus saw Nathanael approaching, he said of him, 'Here truly is an Israelite in whom there is no deceit' " (John 1:47).

I love that! If there is one benefit of being a skeptic, it's that you aren't easily deceived. You are constantly saying to the people around you, "Hey, prove it! Show me you're the real deal." There's just one challenge about acting like you're from the "Show Me State," though. You have to be open, ready, and willing to learn. When you call somebody's bluff, you better be ready if they smack you up side of the head with a mess of truth:

> "How do you know me?" Nathanael asked. Jesus
> answered, "I saw you while you were still under
> the fig tree before Philip called you." (John 1:48)

Isn't it incredible to think that Jesus sees you, right now, holding this book in your hands? Jesus saw you last night, wherever you were (that might *not* be such a good thing, depending on what you were doing). Jesus knows your name, even if you have never told Him your name. He knows where you were just a few minutes ago. So, if you think the NSA has all the intelligence on you or that the IRS has the lowdown on your finances, they've got nothing on God! He's the One who banks all the information about you, and I do mean *all* the information. Jesus knows things about you that you don't even know about yourself! Have you ever said, "I don't know why I did that?" Well, you might not, but Jesus does. He knows the deepest motives of why you act the way you do and even why you *think* the way you do!

When you hear Christians say, "I just love spending time with the Lord," that isn't some syrupy cliché to score points with God. It's all about the *learning*! Their feeling is like you might experience about spending time with Warren Buffet to learn how to invest in the stock market. It would be like hanging out with Blake Shelton to learn about breaking into the country music scene. Or like getting basketball advice from LeBron James or Michael Jordan. The truth is, it would be even more amazing than hanging with all of those mentors, combined! That's a pretty good reason to spend time with Jesus every morning. You just might get some insight into your life!

Our disciple friend Nathanael got the message real quick. Jesus tells Nathanael, "Dawg, I saw you sittin' under that tree, way before you ever came around the corner!" And look at Nate's reaction: "Then Nathanael declared, 'Rabbi, you are the Son of God; you are the king of Israel'" (John 1:49). Once you come face-to-face with the truth of who Jesus Christ is, you are messed up, man—blown away!

Then Jesus gives Nathanael the punchline: "Jesus said, 'You believe because I told you I saw you under the fig tree. You will see greater things than that'" (John 1:50).

God has new, incredible, exciting, deep things
to show you every day, if you will be open to
letting Him show you.

It's all about learning to *learn*, about letting Jesus teach you every single day. For anyone within earshot of Jesus' conversation with Nathanael, they too learned something profound. In Jeremiah 33:3, in fact, God gives us a *promise* about learning:

"Call to Me and I will answer you, and I will tell you great and mighty things, which you do not know" (Jeremiah 33:3, NASB).

When I hear people say, "I just don't know what to do right now," I feel like saying to them, "Have you cried out to God, and asked Him to *show you great and mighty things which you do not know?*" God loves to reveal Himself to you and me and to teach us what we don't know. He's just waiting for us to turn to Him . . . to learn. Ephesians 5:15-17 (ICB) reflects this:

> Be very wise how you live. Don't live like those
> who are not wise. Live wisely. I mean that you
> should use every chance you have for doing
> good, because these are evil times. So don't be
> foolish with your lives. *Learn* what the Lord
> wants you to do. (emphasis mine)

There it is. *Learn what the Lord wants you to do.* God put you on this planet to *learn to become like Jesus.* He is the model He wants us to grow up to be like.

> This learning thing is a big deal with God. In
> fact, I believe God wants us to be
> life-long learners, constantly listening for
> His leading and advice, up until each of us
> takes our last breath.

Long-term Learning

Learning doesn't happen overnight. You don't one day suddenly—ZAP!—become just like Jesus. It's a process, and the process of "spiritual learning" is called "discipleship," which takes an entire lifetime. It will take the rest of our lives for God to build the character qualities of Jesus into you and me. And I hate to tell you this, but there's a good chance the process will have some *pain and failure* involved. In fact, I can pretty much guarantee it!

Still, I encourage you with this: every trial awaits triumph. Every mess awaits a message. Every test awaits a testimony. There was no resurrection without the cross! And God never wastes a hurt. In fact, pain, trials, tribulations, and failure are all a part of God's process of making you complete and useful.

> Often, what you think is destroying you
> is simply God's process of *anointing you*.
> Anointing oil comes from crushing olives until
> the oil flows out.

So when God anoints you, it means He's consecrating you, setting you up to set you apart. Maybe you know exactly what I'm talking about. You're being crushed. You're being squeezed. If so, be encouraged. God is setting you apart, and He's anointing you.

What you think is a setback, is really a *setting apart* for a send out! What you think is a setback, is a set*up* for a comeback!

God wants to use your pains, your hurts, your trials, your tribulations, and your failures to *help others*. So submit your situation to God. He's got you, and He knows what you need, right when you need it. Remember Proverbs 3:5-6:

> Trust in the LORD with all your heart and lean
> not on your own understanding; in all your ways
> submit to him, and he will make your paths
> straight.

That beat-down trying to break you can't keep you down and take you because God's got you. Trust in Him!

There's actually an amazing analogy here to what makes a golf ball special. Early golf balls were made with a smooth outside surface. Over time, people realized that after a ball had been roughed up, dented, and blemished, it was actually able to go further! So the manufacturers started to make them with dimpled outer covers. You can be like a dimpled golf ball. A few rough spots and some beat-downs in your life will make you fly farther!

Most of the time, when we see junk coming at us, we start to freak out. We worry; we wonder what to do. We wonder where we're going. And we usually miss the chance to see it as a learning experience. But James (not the disciple we talked about earlier but the one who was the brother of Jesus) saw problems a bit differently:

> When you have many kinds of troubles, you
> should be full of joy, because you know that
> these troubles test your faith, and this will give
> you patience. . . Then you will be mature and
> complete (James 1:2-4, NCV)

You might be smack in the middle of a lonely, dark, scary alley right now, and it's because God wants to use *you* to be a light and guide for someone else who's headed there.

It's easy to trust God when everything is going great in your life. But the real test of your faith is "What do you do when you run into problems?" Some people are tempted to put on a painfully sad face, mope around, and look like the end of the world has just been announced. Have you met people like that? Yes, problems can seem huge, and there's every reason to make yourself sad about it, but notice the key word, *make*. Your attitude, your disposition, is something you *make* happen! When any of us get down on life and say stuff like "I'm just hangin' on, doin' my best," we show that we still haven't really *learned*.

But I know you won't do that, right? After all, *you* are a game changer! You're like the apostle Paul who said:

> We also have joy with our troubles, because
> we know that these troubles produce patience.
> And patience produces character, and character
> produces hope. (Romans 5:3-4, NCV)

Notice a crucial, three-letter word in this passage: "joy."

Game changers don't wait for conditions to improve. They have learned how to have joy while they are in the middle of troubles. If you want to overflow with *hope* during a horrific trial, then take the entire situation as a learning experience, and start smiling!

I'm not talking about fake happiness or putting on an act. The Bible is telling us that we should have an incredible, unexplainable joy that only God can produce in our hearts. There are millions of people who get joyful when fun stuff happens. That's easy. The people I admire are the ones who stay positive and joyful when they go through a living hell on earth.

"Joy Unspeakable," an old hymn my little church used to sing, drives home the point (you'll have to excuse the "Kingeth Jameseth" sound of the language, but these words just can't be duplicated or imitated; you'll see what I mean):

> I have found His grace is all complete,
> He supplieth every need;
> While I sit and learn at Jesus' feet,
> I am free, yes, free indeed.
>
> It is joy unspeakable and full of glory,
> Full of glory, full of glory;
> It is joy unspeakable and full of glory,
> Oh, the half has never yet been told.

Today, you are going to encounter problems, difficulties, and challenges. You might receive the most devastating news of your life—I hope you don't, but you might. Whatever happens, in that moment, remember two words: *learn* and *joy*. *Learn* the lesson God wants you to learn, and stay *joy*ful. If you do, you will have learned two game-changing attitudes!

Prayer for Learning

Dear Jesus,

I know that becoming a game changer means I have to learn. I need to be constantly open to new things You want me to know. Help me stop being so bull-headed about what happens, and let me always seek to learn more from everybody around me. Most of all, let me hear Your voice and learn to learn directly from You.

In Jesus Name. Amen.

Scriptures to Reflect on

John 14:21
Luke 6:47-48
Hebrews 11:6

Chapter 6

FAVOR

"The pitcher has got only a ball. I've got a bat.
So the percentage in weapons is in my favor and I let
the fellow with the ball do the fretting."

—HANK AARON

Featured Disciple:
James the Less, the one who got to see the risen Jesus first.

---

*"My son, do not forget my teaching, but keep my
commands in your heart, for they will prolong your
life many years and bring you peace and prosperity.
Let love and faithfulness never leave you; bind them
around your neck, write them on the tablet of your
heart. Then you will win favor and a good name in
the sight of God and man."*
Proverbs 3:1-4

Favor is "a gracious, friendly, or obliging act that is freely granted;
friendly or favorable regard; approval or support; partiality;
favoritism; a privilege or concession."
[www.thefreedictionary.com]

In the last few years, I have come to believe that the *favor* of God is more important than I ever realized. I have underestimated the extraordinary benefits of having God's favor shining on my life. His favor is really the *only* thing I need from God for my life.

The Apostle James, son of Alphaeus, was also known as "James the Less" or "James the Little." He is not to be confused with James, the son of Zebedee, one of the "Sons of Thunder" we talked about earlier. This James is the less prominent disciple and is barely mentioned in Scripture. Nevertheless, he was one of the twelve, which is no small honor.

There is one little detail given to us about James, outside of the Gospel accounts, by the apostle Paul in 1 Corinthians 15:7: "Then he appeared to James, then to all the apostles." Don't miss that key word, *then*. I love that! It appears that Jesus, after rising from the dead, went and found the *least* of the disciples, one of the twelve who appears to always be the one "behind the scenes," James the Less, and He appeared to him *first*.

You should be jumping outta your chair right now to shout me down, because this little verse should be one of the most exciting things you've ever heard! Jesus goes and seeks out "the Less." If you think you have never accomplished much in life, if you think you are constantly getting overshadowed by a bunch of greater people, if you feel like you are always the underdog, then this verse is maybe going to become one of your all-time favorites. Jesus appeared *first* to the *least*!

You are never too small in the Kingdom of God to end up receiving the favor of God!

The Details of God's Favor

When something really cool happens to us, we tend to say things like, "What a coincidence!" or "Wow! I am so lucky!" or "The stars aligned!" But let me be very clear on this point: I don't believe coincidence, luck, or alignment of stars is what's in play here. God is. He is at work bestowing favor.

A lot of people—even Christians—believe God isn't very involved in the daily details of our lives anymore, but *they're wrong*. God is involved in more than you could ever imagine!

Many people say, "God created the world and the natural laws that govern it, and now He just lets everything run its course." But I don't buy that at all. I have seen too much evidence of God at work in my own life. I have seen Him totally intervene in situations and change the course of events. When everything was about to "naturally" head off in a certain direction, I have seen God make a radical change that altered what seemed to be the order of natural laws.

God's favor is something each of us should desire in our lives, because favor from God is truly a game changer. Let me tell you a story about favor.

Early in our marriage, Natalie, was diagnosed with endometriosis. Not only was it physically painful, the diagnosis came with the devastating news that most women having her level of endometriosis are unable to conceive and have children. For a new wife who had her heart set on having a family, the news was crushing. It left both of us discouraged and hopeless. On top of that, when the physical pain is so intense that you can't function, the pain, frustration, and discouragement become roadblocks that seem insurmountable. But that is the exact sort of impossible situation which requires God's favor.

God's favor is the special ingredient that changes impossible situations and makes them possible. God specializes in doing the impossible.

Favor by Example

There are many examples of people in the Bible who have found favor with God, not the least of which is Mary, the mother of Jesus. The angel telling Mary that she would give birth to the Christ child is a stunning example of God's favor. It's easy to forget that Mary, because she was found to be pregnant while she was only betrothed, could have been dragged into court, found guilty of breaking the law of Moses, and stoned to death. The Old Testament law as outlined in Deuteronomy 22:20-21 is completely clear on this point:

> If, however, the charge is true and no proof of
> the young woman's virginity can be found, she
> shall be brought to the door of her father's house

and there the men of her town shall stone her to death.

Talk about an open and shut case! Mary the mother of Jesus would have been doomed the minute anyone found out she was pregnant. This was the kind of thing that made the evening news in Jerusalem. Mary would have been the focus of a scandal of the highest proportions. Gossip would have run rampant. Many people would exaggerate the facts and make things worse by adding to the story. *Jerry Springer, The View,* or *The Talk* would have loved this story. But what changed the plight of Mary— and the course of history? What reversed this impossible situation even before it could become a scandal? Brace yourself, because it's the very thing you should be desiring every day for yourself: "And the angel said to her, 'Do not be afraid, Mary, for you have found favor with God'" (Luke 1:30).

Mary found favor with God! God's favor took a law of the land and somehow made it *not* apply.

Favor is one of the most incredible, game-changing things you can acquire in your life. God's favor changes the impossible!

But Mary wasn't the first person in the Bible to be blessed with God's favor. You may recall the Old Testament dude named Daniel (if not, you need to go read his book called . . . of all things, Daniel). He experienced some outlandish stories of courage, prayer, character, insight, and victory. But the most important thing you will notice in Daniel's book is . . . *favor*.

While Daniel and his friends are held in exile in Babylon, Daniel is chosen to serve the king of the oppressing nation, and Daniel piled up a whole bunch of blessings because of it:

> Then the king gave Daniel high honors and
> many great gifts, and made him ruler over the
> whole province of Babylon and chief prefect over
> all the wise men of Babylon. (Daniel 2:48)

You might be tempted to say something like, "Aw, dog, that's just a coincidence. Daniel was probably such a cool hipster that he just naturally won people over. He was legit."

Uh . . . no.

Almighty God, Jehovah Jireh, The Provider, was working behind the scenes for Daniel. This guy had found favor with God, and in turn, God brought him favor in the eyes of the leaders: "Now God had brought Daniel into favor and goodwill of the chief of the eunuchs" (Daniel 1:9, NKJV).

Daniel had been taken into captivity and basically enslaved by the Babylonian king, and yet, God's *favor* turned the situation into a *benefit* for Daniel, full of blessing, gifts, and honor. God's favor definitely changes the outcome.

God's favor can string together a bunch of seemingly unrelated events into an astounding chain reaction that brings about a miracle.

Perhaps the best part of this is that God's favor doesn't just happen to people in the Bible. Check out this story.

In 1858, a Boston Sunday school teacher named Edward Kimball led a local shoe store clerk to give his life to Jesus Christ. That clerk was Dwight L. Moody who became one of the greatest evangelists in American history. What a chain reaction Mr. Kimball set off!

In 1879, while Moody preached in England, the heart of a pastor named F. B. Meyer was set on fire. He later came to an American college campus to preach, and under Meyer's preaching, a student by the name of Wilbur Chapman was saved. Chapman began work in the YMCA and employed a former baseball player named Billy Sunday to help with evangelistic work. Billy Sunday held a revival in Charlotte, North Carolina where his preaching inspired thirty businessmen to start a day of prayer for Charlotte.

In May 1934, a farmer lent the men some land to use for their prayer meeting, and the leader of the businessmen, Vernon Patterson, prayed that "out of Charlotte the Lord would raise up someone to preach the Gospel to the ends of the earth." The businessmen then called for another evangelistic meeting and asked Mordecai Ham, a fiery Southern evangelist to preach. Ham shattered the complacency of church-going Charlotte. The farmer who provided his land for the prayer meeting was Franklin Graham and his son, Billy, became a Christian during the meeting.

Coincidence? Ain't no way you're convincing me that there is such a thing.

Favor above All

Doctors can give you their professional opinions. Specialists can say you'll never recover. The best minds in the world may proclaim that yours is a hopeless case. But the favor of God can make every one of their declarations completely irrelevant!

If you have trouble thinking of how God's favor works, Kobe Bryant, the legendary basketball player for the LA Lakers, gave us a great way to look at it when he said, "These young guys are playing checkers. I'm out there playing chess."

When you have the favor of God, you switch from checkers to chess. God looks farther ahead than you can ever look, so He can give you the breaks, the "coincidences," the strategies, and the insights you need. You may see only the next move immediately in front of you, but God sees the complex of steps needed to solve your problem, and He can make whatever move it takes to orchestrate the whole thing.

I'll never forget the day my wife came walking down the hallway of our little house, looking like she would explode with joy. Without a word, she presented me with a pregnancy test showing that—endometriosis or not—we were going to have a baby!

We laughed and cried, and then we laughed and cried. Our miracle baby, Kylie Andrea Sierra Hearn (KASH), was born on November 20, 2000. Every time I look at Kylie, I remember all over again the *favor* of God in our lives. Kylie's life is a tangible witness of His amazing favor!

People will try to talk you out of believing in God's favor. You might even do it to yourself at times. Besides the luck and coincidence jabber, there are other ways people disdain God's favor. Some will tell you that "you have to make it happen." Or you'll hear quotes like, "If it's going to be, it's up to me."

Yes, it is true that you have to take some sort of action. God gave you a body and a brain and a heart to use. He doesn't want you to just go sit on a hill, staring up at heaven, waiting for Him to answer your prayers by parting the clouds and zapping up a miracle for you. Each of us must do the best we can. Once that's done, though, we trust God to give the favor we need.

If you ignore God's favor, you will feel like the weight of making things "work" is totally on your shoulders. You might even wonder, at the very core of your faith, if God even hears or answers your prayers.

But I know that won't happen to you. Because *you* are a game changer!

Right now, I hope you are ready to boldly claim God's favor in your life, that your spirit will rise up and claim what He wants for you! That doesn't mean God will get rid of every bump in the road. In fact, the bumps might never go away. You may live a life full of challenges, difficulties, and heartbreaking losses. I am pretty sure Daniel didn't think being held captive in a foreign country was much of a picnic! But in the middle of his captivity, in the middle of a wicked king's aggression, Daniel found favor with the leaders around him. And in the face of circumstantial evidence that suggested the mother of Jesus had been promiscuous and deserved to be stoned, it was God's favor that protected her and gave her the phenomenal job description of raising the Son of God to manhood!

So, now, please do *me* a favor. From this day forward, vow that *you will seek God's favor*, you will *watch for God's favor*, you will *never underestimate God's favor*, and you will *give God all the credit* when you have a sneakin' suspicion that something that just happened was a total God thing!

Prayer for Favor

Dear Jesus,

I pray for boatloads of Your favor so I can be a game changer! Right now, I ask You to pour out Your favor on my life. Please give me favor with people I don't know, in places I've never been, in areas I'm not even thinking about. Let there be an abundance of Your favor in my life, not just to provide me with things I want but to help me advance the Gospel to people who really need to hear about You. I want to walk in Your favor today— and every day.

In Jesus Name. Amen.

Scriptures to Reflect on

Genesis 39:3-4
Psalm 30:5
Psalm 5:1

Chapter 7

PERSEVERANCE

"I've experienced the highest of highs and lowest of lows. I think to really appreciate anything, you have to be at both ends of the spectrum. I've always joked about Joe Montana not appreciating his Super Bowls nearly as much as I do, because he never lost one. *We lost three before we got one.*"

—JOHN ELWAY

Featured Disciple:
Simon the Zealot, the disciple who persevered against evil.

"Therefore, since we have been justified through faith, we have peace with God through our Lord Jesus Christ, through whom we have gained access by faith into this grace in which we now stand. And we boast in the hope of the glory of God. Not only so, but we also glory in our sufferings, because we know that suffering produces perseverance; perseverance, character; and character, hope."
Romans 5:1-4

Perseverance is "steady persistence in adhering to a course of action, a belief, or a purpose; steadfastness; withstanding discouragement or difficulty."
[www.thefreedictionary.com]

The Bible doesn't tell us much about Simon the Zealot, one of the twelve disciples. In fact, he is only mentioned three times in the Gospels, and even then, he is just *on the list*. We don't have much to go on, except for his name, "Simon the Zealot." The more you think about that name, the more you may find yourself wondering about this guy. Very few people have a name that communicates how passionate he or she is about life's greatest challenges.

Bible scholars are at odds about Simon the Zealot. Some believe he was a key leader in a band of political activists called "Zealots," known especially for their hatred of the Romans. Others think the name was just a description of his passion and zeal for telling people about Jesus. Given that the Zealots were such a major influence in the days of Jesus, though, it's pretty easy to imagine that Jesus called a leader in this group of "haters" to take up the "Gospel of Love" Jesus taught.

The Zealots were consumed with trying to eliminate Roman rule and pagan practices, even by force and violence if necessary. The first-century Jewish historian Josephus had a lot to say about the Zealots. According to him, they were a force to be reckoned with for Rome and its leaders. These guys were no joke.

So, I think of Simon as a Zealot, and it was a stroke of genius for Jesus to put Matthew, a Jewish tax collector *for* Rome, on the same team with a leader of a sect that despised Rome and everything about the Romans. That one crucial choice shows how much Jesus came to unify, not divide, people. Jesus demonstrated that His gospel is not a political calling.

God is neither a Democrat nor a Republican. Jesus is love, and His love transcends all political ties. One thing that is no doubt true about Simon the Zealot, though, is that he had learned to persevere in his passionate quests. Whatever he may have thought about the Romans and grinding them into the dust, his persevering character is a positive attribute because—news flash!—unfortunately, "perseverance" means there is something to persevere through. And we all face those some-things—like Natalie and her endometriosis. Most people have no clue that she still suffers from this disease because she perseveres, with God's help, daily.

Persevere When It Hurts

But we all have our issues, don't we? Everybody has a hidden hurt. Whether it's a physical, emotional, or relational pain, we all have wounds. If you suffer with a medical problem or chronic pain, my heart goes out to you. I feel for you; I can relate. You see, I was in a car wreck when I was twenty years old, and I have suffered with chronic neck pain ever since. Doctors have diagnosed me with bulging disks, degenerative disks, and arthritis. It affects everything in my daily life, and I mean *everything*.

I have refused, so far, to take any high-powered pain killers, because I don't want to end up being "that guy" with a blank look in my eye and slurred speech, but I am a pretty heavy user of Ibuprofen. I have been to chiropractors, MD's, DO's, and everything in between. Although epidural injections give me some temporary relief, I have to limit how often I receive that treatment because it is so invasive. It requires sticking a needle into my spinal fluids and injecting an anti-inflammatory drug, and it has to be administered while I am under an x-ray machine. Recently, doctors tried another procedure called

Radiofrequency Ablation in which the doctor burns the nerves in half in the affected C-Spine area by the use of needles and radio frequency activity. (Are you grossed out yet?) But as traumatic as the procedure was, it didn't help at all.

Even writing this brief description arouses the feeling I often have, which is, "Lord, why don't you just shut me down now, and let me come up to heaven and hang with you?" It's that bad. In fact, the only way I can write a sermon (or a book!) on the computer is to sit in a special chair tilted "just so" and to have the computer monitor mounted high on the wall, so I don't have to tweak my neck. I must confess that as I'm writing this book, I'm in excruciating pain. It feels like a hot, electric fork is stabbing into my neck and piercing my spine. Pretty ridiculous, huh?

Now let me be clear. I don't share this information for sympathy or just to relate a sob story. No, I tell you this so you'll know I understand pain and what it takes to persevere in spite of it.

On many Sunday mornings, I preach three services, then race down to the US Airways arena for the Phoenix Suns chapel service, and my neck is in so much pain, I can't even move my head. A lot of people don't notice, but there are times while I'm speaking that the pain is so overpowering my eyes fill with tears. But there's really not much I can do about it. When you have pain like that, you just have to learn to live with it. So, believe me, if that's you, too, I am completely sorry. I have so much compassion for you that I "blanket pray" for people like you all the time who suffer like I do. I know how horrible it is.

Now I have much greater compassion for people who suffer with pain than I did before my accident. But in one way or another, everybody has to deal with pain. You would be surprised at how many great athletes have to "play through" the pain. At the risk of overusing quotes by Kobe Bryant of the Los Angeles Lakers (especially since I am the team pastor for the Phoenix Suns), Kobe gave us a behind-the-scenes glimpse into what playing through pain is like when he said:

> I've played with IVs before, during and after
> games. I've played with a broken hand, a
> sprained ankle, a torn shoulder, a fractured
> tooth, a severed lip, and a knee the size of a
> softball. I don't miss 15 games because of a toe
> injury that everybody knows wasn't that serious
> in the first place.

If there was ever a description of "perseverance" for an athlete, Kobe's would definitely make it into the top ten! Perseverance is all about being tough, in spite of the incredible pain wracking your body, your mind, or your emotions.

The apostle Paul must have experienced a problem with some sort of chronic pain. Many people have speculated that he had trouble with his eyes, since he was temporarily blinded by the flash of light when Jesus appeared to him on the Damascus road. Whatever the specific problem, though, something in Paul's body caused him great difficulty—so much so, that he begged God to take it away:

> Therefore, in order to keep me from becoming
> conceited, I was given a thorn in my flesh, a
> messenger of Satan, to torment me. Three times
> I pleaded with the Lord to take it away from me.

> But he said to me, "My grace is sufficient for
> you, for my power is made perfect in weakness."
> Therefore I will boast all the more gladly about
> my weaknesses, so that Christ's power may
> rest on me. That is why, for Christ's sake, *I
> delight* in weaknesses, in insults, in hardships,
> in persecutions, in difficulties. For when I am
> weak, then I am strong. (2 Corinthians 12:7-10,
> emphasis mine)

Did you catch that little bit of craziness? Paul said he *delights* in weaknesses, insults, hardships, persecutions, and difficulties! There are a lot of words that come to mind when I think of that little list of atrocities, but *delight* is definitely not one of them. How can someone do that? How can you find a way to delight in things that are absolutely not delightful?

Persevere When It's Hard

The Old Testament King David lived through one hardship after another. He was hunted down by his predecessor, Saul, who once tried to spear him to a wall. David had a moral failure with a married woman that turned a million times worse when he had her husband murdered. The child the woman conceived by David got sick and died. One of David's daughters was raped by one of his sons. A rebellious son named Absalom tried to dethrone David and was killed at the height of his rebellion. And that's not even everything on David's list! He went through crushing adversity, difficulty, and failure, yet he wrote these amazing words in Psalm 37:4: "Take delight in the Lord, and he will give you the desires of your heart."

David never lost sight of the secret to a great life. He didn't find his "delight" in the things of this world. He found his delight *in the Lord*!

Delighting in the Lord was a consistent theme in everything David did. David even went so far as to say it was the reason why he could continually rebound from devastating events. Check out what David wrote in Psalm 37:23-24:

> The Lord makes firm the steps of the one who
> delights in him; though he may stumble, he will
> not fall, for the Lord upholds him with his hand.

Are you starting to notice a pattern here? You will see weaknesses, insults, hardships, persecutions, and difficulties in an excitingly different light if you learn to "take delight in the Lord." It's actually the secret way in which God will give you the desires of your heart. You simply need to delight yourself in Jesus!

Delightful Perseverance

You might ask, "How exactly am I supposed to do all this delighting in God? What specific ways are there for me to do this? Would it surprise you to know that the Bible itself gives us a very specific answer? (I hope not.) Here it is:

> I delight greatly in the Lord; my soul rejoices in
> my God. For he has clothed me with garments
> of salvation and arrayed me in a robe of his
> righteousness, as a bridegroom adorns his head

like a priest, and as a bride adorns herself with
her jewels. (Isaiah 61:10)

Why do we delight ourselves in the Lord? It's because Jesus
has forgiven us all of our sins! According to Psalm 103:12, God
has separated our sins as far as the east is from the west—in
other words, a complete and total separation from us.

Our sins no longer define us. They no longer define our character. They are not a description of who we are. They are forgiven!
And there isn't just a void or vacuum left behind. Jesus puts a robe
of righteousness on us, a robe of *his* righteousness, and that is way
better than any wimpy righteousness we could drum up on our
own!

So, let's summarize:

- How do you persevere, when everything within you
  wants to quit, when you are facing an absolute brick wall,
  when you see no way to go forward, when you feel like
  .the thorn in the flesh is just too hard to bear for even one
  more day?
- You *delight* yourself in the Lord and in the reality that He
  has clothed you with a *robe of righteousness*. Then you let
  that fact overwhelm you with the love, grace, mercy, and
  faithfulness of God!

I love the inspiring perseverance story about Randy Pausch.
Randy (October 23, 1960–July 25, 2008) was an American pro-
fessor of computer science at Carnegie Mellon University in
Pittsburgh. Pausch learned that he had pancreatic cancer in
September 2006, and in August 2007, he was given a terminal
diagnosis: "three to six months of good health left." He gave an

upbeat lecture titled, "The Last Lecture: Really Achieving Your Childhood Dream" on September 18, 2007, at Carnegie Mellon, which went viral on YouTube. Pausch died of complications from the cancer on July 25, 2008. One of the statements from his "Last Lecture" is a favorite of mine and shows his determination and perseverance:

> The brick walls are there for a reason. The brick walls are not there to keep us out. The brick walls are there to give us a chance to show how badly we want something. Because the brick walls are there to stop the people who don't want it badly enough. They're there to stop the other people.

That upbeat lecture is still inspiring students, businesspeople, entrepreneurs, CEO's, and athletes *to persevere*.

Who gives you the *power* to face something as devastating as cancer? The Lord Jesus does with His unfailing love, faithfulness, and righteousness. If you try to manufacture that kind of determination and perseverance on your own, you might be like me if I try—ready to throw in the towel when things get really insurmountable. You might feel like you just can't go on.

But you won't.

Because you won't forget that you are a game changer.

The world has never seen anyone as determined as you! You can show the naysayers, the doubters, and the haters that they shouldn't have drank that *Hater-ade*! You *will* persevere, even when everything and everybody says you should throw in the towel and give up. You *will* delight yourself in the fact that you are suffering under weaknesses, insults, hardships, persecutions, and difficulties. You *will* delight because you know these things are producing a toughness in you that will be unmatched by others. You stand proud, "because we know that suffering produces perseverance; perseverance, character; and character, hope" (Romans 5:3-4).

As Winston Churchill said in one of his most famous speeches:

> Never give in. Never give in. Never, never,
> never, never—in nothing, great or small, large
> or petty—never give in, except to convictions
> of honor and good sense. Never yield to force.
> Never yield to the apparently overwhelming
> might of the enemy. (from *Never Give In!: The
> Best of Winston Churchill's Speeches*)

And like the famous baseball slugger, Babe Ruth, once said, simply, "It's hard to beat the person who never gives up."

Right now, even if you're lying in a hospital bed, sitting in a wheelchair, completely incapacitated in some way, unable to dance—or maybe even walk—would you please, in your mind's eye, envision yourself leaping and dancing in celebration, because when you do, you are delighting in all the *junk* that has come your way. It has made you the amazing person you are. And congratulations, because you are a game changer in every sense of the word! You are more amazing than words can even describe. Believe it! Please!

Don't you dare—ever, ever, ever—think of giving up!

Prayer for Perseverance

Dear Jesus,

You know I have felt like giving up. When the winds of adversity and difficulty blow this strong, I want to throw in the towel. I find myself looking at the mountain I must climb, and I want to give up. I really, really do. But over and over in Your Word, You constantly tell me never to give up. Even Your own Son, Jesus, persevered when He faced torture and a grueling death on the cross. So, Lord, I pray that You will fill me with perseverance. Help me become a person who never, never, never ever gives up! Fill me full of determination and tenacity like the great athletes and coaches. Fill me with perseverance like the great heroes of faith in the Bible. Let me be known for my great perseverance under pressure and adversity.

In Jesus Name. Amen!

Scriptures to Reflect on

James 1:12
Hebrews 12:1-2
Galatians 6:9

Chapter 8

DREAMS

"Never underestimate the power of dreams and the influence of the human spirit. We are all the same in this notion: The potential for greatness lives within each of us."

—WILMA RUDOLPH, USA GOLD MEDALIST IN TRACK AND FIELD, NAMED "FASTEST WOMAN IN THE WORLD" IN THE 1960'S

Featured Disciple:
John, one of the "Sons of Thunder," one of the disciples closest to Jesus and writer of Revelation, a book of vision.

"God can do anything, you know—far more than you could ever imagine or guess or request in your wildest dreams! He does it not by pushing us around but by working within us, his Spirit deeply and gently within us."
Ephesians 3:20 (THE MESSAGE)

Dreams are "a wild fancy or hope; a condition or achievement that is longed for; an aspiration; one that is exceptionally gratifying, excellent, or beautiful."
[www.thefreedictionary.com]

What is your dream for your life? Have you thought about that very much?

Natalie and I have had many God-given dreams, but our most amazing dreams have to do with our children. As they grow up, we find ourselves talking more than ever about big dreams for our kids.

The God of Dreams

I think God loves it when we dream big dreams. From early on, Natalie and I have had big dreams about our family. Much of what we envisioned seemed impossible, a few dreams may have even seemed silly, and, possibly to some people, others would appear irresponsible and poorly planned. But that's why they're *dreams*. Ideas like that usually become dreams because a huge obstacle lies in the way that will keep it from happening naturally. Dreams are those crazy, ridiculous, pie-in-the-sky notions that have no way of becoming a reality—at least from what you and I can tell. If you can figure out how something is going to be possible, then it's not a dream; it's a goal. Dreams form when you reach past the impossible to the outrageous but still believe something inside of you says it really can happen. Dreams make our hearts soar.

Wilma Rudolph had a dream not only to become an Olympic athlete but to win a gold medal. Her dream seemed ridiculous beyond reason. Why? To start with, Wilma was born prematurely, weighing in at a 4.5-pound birth weight. She was the twentieth of twenty-two siblings, which surely created enormous challenges. The young Wilma Rudolph developed infantile paralysis as a result of polio at age four. By nine-years-old, she had a twisted leg and foot from the polio, and at twelve, she had a bout with scarlet fever.

Yet in 1952, Rudolph began copying her older sister's aspirations by playing basketball on the high school team, and as a result, Ed Temple, Tennessee State University track and field coach, "discovered" her. This was a huge break, since he had trained many athletes who went on to great recognition. By the time Wilma was sixteen-years-old, she attended the 1956 Melbourne Olympic games and came home with a bronze medal in the 4 x 100 relay. Many people would probably be satisfied with such an amazing accomplishment, but not Wilma. She still wanted to win the gold!

Four years later, Rudolph went to the Olympic games again, this time in Rome, and came away with *three* Olympic gold medals—in the 100-meter, 200-meter, and the 4 x 100 meter relays. Even more amazing, she won the gold—with eighty thousand spectators watching and at temperatures inside the Stadio Olimpico reaching 110 degrees—running the 100-meter dash in an amazing eleven seconds flat. She achieved her oversized dreams despite starting life barely able to walk on a twisted foot and leg.

Although I don't know what handicap you have to manage every day, I hope your heart is bursting with great expectations and wildly crazy dreams. If Wilma Rudolph can overcome her depressing, debilitating, devastating obstacles and go on to win Olympic gold medals, then you and I should take good notes. God loves to reverse all the predictions and make miracles happen!

The first disciple Jesus called was a dude named John. He was the other half of "the Sons of Thunder" we talked about earlier. John was also among the three disciples closest to Jesus, making up the famous trio of "Peter, James, and John." John wrote the gospel that bears his name and three letters called First, Second, and Third John, but he is probably most famous for the loony dream which he transcribed into a book called "The Revelation of Jesus Christ." Most of us refer to it as the book of Revelation. (Please note: there is no "s" on the end of the book of Revelation—I said it wrong for years!)

Aside from the fact that John wrote an entire book based on the visions Jesus Christ gave directly to him, there is other evidence that he was a big dreamer. Although John does not write about himself by name in his gospel, he does refer to himself four times with a now-famous phrase, "the disciple Jesus loved." There is a beautiful confidence in that.

If you are going to dream big dreams for God, the secret is for you to have great confidence in the love God has for you.

Dreams are birthed in confidence. Whether or not you like Donald Trump, when you watch him in action on television, you quickly recognize a man who is extremely confident in his abilities. The same should be true for every believer in Jesus. When you cultivate a confidence that comes from believing in the love Jesus has for you, you will start to have dreams that are much bigger than anything you could ever come up with by yourself.

Big Dreams, Baby Dreams

I've told you about Kylie, our miracle who was born in 2000, but we (literally) birthed another miracle after her. Our awesome son, Josiah, was born in 2003. Natalie's condition with endometriosis had given us no hope of ever having children, but God provided us with, not one, but two miracle babies. At that, though, we pretty much figured we were destined to be a "fun-filled family of four," and our childbearing years for Natalie were done. That's when God birthed another dream in our hearts.

At the time, we were heavily involved in missions work on the eastern horn of Africa, building wells for poor villages that didn't have clean drinking water. As a result of our work, we discovered a key principle:

If you want to see God make your dreams come true and want Him to provide a miracle for those dreams to happen, you must be open to *giving back* and doing something great for Him.

It was during our time of "giving back" that God spoke to my heart. He impressed on me to do something that had never crossed my mind before. Not only that, He separately led Natalie in the same way. It was crazy but also very clear: we should *adopt* a baby. We could see that God was leading us to enlarge our family to include a third child, but we had no idea how.

Either an international or domestic adoption would cost far more than the money we had available.

Nevertheless, we explained the idea to Kylie and Josiah, who were six and eight years old at the time, and they were totally excited about it. We said it was an "impossible" dream because we didn't have the $20,000 to $50,000 it would cost. We weren't even close! But there was no question God had put this dream in our hearts.

Lots of people encouraged us to become foster parents. This would allow us to adopt a foster child, and the state would be responsible for the entire process. Other people said we should raise money for our eventual adoption, but we didn't feel comfortable doing that. Since we were on staff at a church, we didn't want people to divert their offerings to our own personal cause. The impossibility didn't go away.

When you can't see a way for your dreams to come true, that's when you should watch for the way God will work it out.

We started taking the courses required for certification to become foster parents. However, the class instructor offered a reality check when she explained that adopting a foster child is a high-risk option. It is common that, at some point, the birth mother could take the baby back (once the state deems her "healthy"), even after you have invested years with the child.

Natalie and I prayed about it and felt like we were pursuing a path that God didn't want us to. The dream seemed farther away than ever. After four years and no clear direction on how to bring about the dream, we started to feel like giving up. In fact, I told a friend at church one Sunday: "God would literally have to drop a baby into our laps for this to happen." Little did we know that was pretty much what God had in mind!

One of the most exciting things you can say and pray to God is, "Lord, you are going to have to drop this in my lap for it to happen." If you say that to God, you better get your lap ready to receive!

The late Martin Luther King Jr. is famous for his audacious dream:

> I have a *dream* that my four little children will one day live in a nation where they will not be judged by the color of their skin but by the content of their character.

Rev. King's dream moved into reality through the sacrifice and the passion by which he lived his life but also by the promises he felt God had given him.

The Bible is full of great stories about people who had a life-changing dream, but one of my favorites reminds me of the Led Zeplin song, "Stairway to Heaven." As a result of the dream in which he saw a ladder reaching to heaven, Jacob renamed an entire city.

He had run into some severe family issues (can you relate?) and had to move out of town in a hurry. Around sunset, he reached a place that looked good for an overnight stop, but in his haste to get out of Dodge, he hadn't even packed a pillow. As a substitute, Jacob found a smooth stone to put under his head as he lay down to sleep.

That night, Jacob had a psychedelic dream in which he saw a stairway going from the place he was sleeping up to the gates of heaven. A bunch of angels skittered up and down this heavenly staircase, and the Lord stood at the top. He said to Jacob:

> I am the Lord, the God of your father Abraham and the God of Isaac. I will give you and your descendants the land on which you are lying. Your descendants will be like the dust of the earth, and you will spread out to the west and to the east, to the north and to the south. All peoples on earth will be blessed through you and your offspring. I am with you and will watch over you wherever you go, and I will bring you back to this land. I will not leave you until I have done what I have *promised* you. (Genesis 28:13-15, emphasis mine)

Great dreams from God will always include *promises* you can claim as you walk through the difficulties and trials that always accompany a great dream.

When Jacob woke up, he took action, based on what God had told him in the dream:

> "Surely the Lord is in this place, and I was
> not aware of it." He was afraid and said, "How
> awesome is this place! This is none other than
> the house of God; this is the gate of heaven."
> Early the next morning Jacob took the stone he
> had placed under his head and set it up as a pillar
> and poured oil on top of it. He called that place
> Bethel, though the city used to be called Luz.
> (Genesis 28:16-19)

Jacob's renaming is an indication of the gigantic change that occurred because of his dream. Great dreams cause huge shifts to happen. They cause things to change in amazing ways. And take note that the first thing Jacob did was honor God for giving him this amazing dream:

> Then Jacob made a vow, saying, "If God will be
> with me and will watch over me on this journey
> I am taking and will give me food to eat and
> clothes to wear so that I return safely to my
> father's household, then the Lord will be my
> God and this stone that I have set up as a pillar
> will be God's house, and of all that you give me I
> will give you a tenth." (Genesis 28:20-22)

After Jacob received the dream from God, he committed to three things, the three S's of a God-given dream: he committed to God his *salvation*, his *story*, and his *salary*. What do I mean by that? Jacob devoted his life to God (*then the Lord will be my God*); he claimed his dream as a testimony of what God had done (*this stone that I have set up as a pillar will be God's house*); and he committed his financial needs to God's provision by tithing on his income (*of all that you give me I will give you a tenth*).

If you want to see God do amazing things in your life, commit to Him your salvation, your story, and your salary, and watch what happens.

Natalie and I received our dream from God and had committed to Him our salvation, story, and salary. Then we waited to see how God would turn our dream into reality.

On Wednesday (three days after I had told my friend that "God would have to drop a baby in our laps"), the receptionist at our church answered the phone and walked down the hall to my office to tell me about it.

"Pastor Travis," she explained. "There's a lady on the phone, who is the friend of a friend of a friend of a lady who is seven months pregnant. She can't keep her baby, and she's looking for a good family for her baby. Can you talk to her? And by the way, the lady on the phone's name is . . . Natalie." Not only does God perform miracles, but He's funny too!

I called this Natalie back, and it turns out she was also a pastor's wife at a church in the Phoenix area. Natalie told me about a young woman in their church who was seven months pregnant.

As my receptionist had said, the woman couldn't keep her baby because she had four other children, and she just wasn't in a good position to keep this one. My heart welled up with compassion for this young lady, thinking about the difficulties she must have already encountered in raising four children.

After my conversation with the other Natalie, I walked to my Natalie's office and told her about the phone call. We were both trippin' with excitement about the possibility of adopting this child and overflowing with feelings for this birth mom and what she'd been through.

Natalie and I stepped outside and called Natalie again. I asked her to tell us more about the mom and her other children. Natalie explained that the children were all beautiful, smart, and healthy. She said, "The mother's name is Amber, and I really think it would be great if you two could meet her as soon as possible."

If God gives you an amazing dream, it always will require you to have grace, compassion, love, and acceptance. God never births a dream in you from wrong attitudes.

I will never forget how my Natalie and I felt in that moment. We huddled under one of the shade structures outside the church, so other people wouldn't see us talking and crying. A flood of emotion poured over us, and we wept for joy and excitement over how God was miraculously putting together our dream. We were overjoyed beyond our wildest dreams but also afraid to let our hearts completely go there until we knew the adoption was really going to happen. We told the other Natalie we wanted to talk with Amber as soon as possible.

Have you ever been afraid to believe your miracle is *finally* happening? That was exactly how we felt! We were almost afraid to breathe. We diluted our excitement because we couldn't quite believe this miracle could be unfolding right in front of our eyes. In the back of my mind, I was thinking, "Is God *really* going to drop a child right into our laps? Is He actually going to answer that crazy prayer of ours? Is He *really*?"

Natalie put us in touch with Amber that day. Amber explained why she couldn't keep the baby and how she'd been praying about finding a God-fearing home to adopt her child.

I asked Amber if she could meet with Natalie and me, and she suggested, "How about if you come down to my church *tonight* and meet?" We couldn't say *yes* fast enough! God wasn't wasting any time!

When God makes you wait and takes you through an agonizing time of feeling like your dreams will never happen, that is just setting you up for the huge miracle that's coming.

Natalie and I drove to the other church that night, and we— my Natalie, the other one, Amber, and I—sat in a circle and talked for a couple of hours. We held hands, prayed, and finally

Amber said, "I feel really good about this; God is answering my prayers!" We left the building that night, blown away at how much God had accomplished for us *in just one day*!

If your miracle seems far away as you hold this book in your hands, I want you to picture our story in your mind. In less than twenty-four hours, our dream that seemed impossibly far away suddenly was happening.

As we began working out details of the adoption, we realized all the legal paperwork would still be very expensive, and Natalie and I were already in difficult financial straits. How would we ever come up with more than $20,000 to pay for a lawyer and legal fees in just eight weeks? Panic started to set in as we realized we had another major obstacle to overcome. But guess what: God had another beautiful solution!

Leading a Suns chapel service a few days later, I struck up a conversation with a kindly lady named Kathy Pidgeon, who is one of the minority owners of the Phoenix Suns. I was so excited about the adoption possibility, I shared the miraculous details about how it had all unfolded.

I think God loves it when we share the details
of great things He is doing in our lives—one
of the three S's, our *story*.

The God-ordained irony of my sharing the story with this particular lady was that, unbeknownst to me, I was talking to a lawyer! And not just any sort of lawyer. She was an *adoption lawyer* who had been handling local adoptions for thirty years! Touched by my story and convinced God was at work, this lady's eyes teared up, and she said, "Travis, I have goose bumps all over me, and I just feel so strongly this baby is supposed to be yours, and . . . this *is God*! I will represent you *pro bono*—for *free*. You won't pay me one penny to get this adoption done."

I remember thinking, "Okay, God, now you're just showin' off!"

I researched this lawyer's background and found out that she was one of the top attorneys in all of Arizona for adoptions. When God shows off, He shows off big-time!

Our lovely new daughter, Jazzlyn Grace Hearn, was born on August 13, 2009 and was welcomed into our family with hearts overflowing with love. When we look at Jazzlyn, we are staring at yet another miracle!

When God gives you a dream for your life—an impossible idea that is way beyond anything you can imagine—He also loves to supernaturally provide the perfect resources and circumstances that only He can, to make your dream a reality.

You, Too

Reading the miracle story of our adopting *Jazzy*, you might be tempted to think, "Okay, Pastor Travis, that's nothing but one more example of how everything always seems to go your way. You may have gotten the big miracle, but that will never happen for me!"

You might think huge dreams can never come true for you. Perhaps you once had a big dream for your life, but it got crushed. Maybe someone decided you were too reckless, too poor, too stupid, too unhealthy, too untalented, too ugly, too clueless, too timid, or too damaged for your dreams to ever come true. You might have suffered a setback and decided the best thing for you would be to simply give up on your dreams.

But I say, "No Way!" You're not going to give up your dreams that easily. You do not get to throw in the towel on your dream. No, my friend, not today. And I think, by now, you know why: You are one gutsy game changer!

Here's what you do to salvage your dream. Grab a piece of paper and a pencil, and find a quiet place where you can be alone for a while. Then just start writing. You might even want to write in the margins of this book. Wherever, though, write out the dreams for your life. Even if you are bed-ridden, bankrupt, burned out, or bummed out, God has a dream for your life that will blow you away! And today, you are going to write it down, and you will keep refining it and adding to it and asking God to pave a way for it to happen. You are going to claim this verse for yourself, every single day:

> Now to Him who is able to do exceedingly
> abundantly above all that we ask or think,
> according to the power that works in us!
> (Ephesians 3:20, NKJV)

You might think you are asking God to do more than is possible, but the truth is, God has a dream for your life that is exceedingly, abundantly *above anything you could possibly dream up*. You're like an ant trying to understand the Internet. It's just way past your capabilities. And that's one reason why it's going to be so awesome. Today, a brand new life is being launched for you, a life full of dreams for the future. Get out there, and start asking God to birth it in your heart and to make it an amazing adventure for you!

Dream, dream, and dream some more! Commit to God your *salvation*, your *story*, and your *salary*, and watch what happens. Pray this chapter's prayer with everything you've got because you are now ready to watch Jesus accomplish dreams beyond belief in your life.

Prayer for Dreams

Dear Jesus,

There are lots of "dream stealers" in my life—sometimes people, sometimes circumstances, sometimes difficulties. And Lord, I have to admit, sometimes those dream stealers have caused me to put my dreams on the shelf and to give up on believing they could ever become a reality. But starting today, I am taking those dreams down from the shelf. I am going to remember that I am the "disciple that Jesus loves." I am going to grasp that bold confidence I have in Your love, Jesus, and I am going to let it propel me to dream greater and greater dreams! Help me become a dreamer without bounds. Give me renewed faith in the dreams that *You* have laid upon my heart.

In Jesus Name. Amen.

Scriptures to Reflect on

Luke 18:1-4
2 Chronicles 15:7
Numbers 12:6

Chapter 9

CHARACTER

"Don't walk through life just playing football. Don't walk through life just being an athlete. Athletics will fade. Character and integrity and really making an impact on someone's life, that's the ultimate vision, that's the ultimate goal—bottom line."

—RAY LEWIS, BALTIMORE RAVENS,
ALL-STAR DEFENSIVE LINEBACKER

Featured Disciple:
Jude, the deep disciple who warned against twisting the gospel.

"So don't lose a minute in building on what you've been given, complementing your basic faith with good character, spiritual understanding, alert discipline, passionate patience, reverent wonder, warm friendliness, and generous love, each dimension fitting into and developing the others."
2 Peter 1: 5 (THE MESSAGE)

Character is "a description of a person's attributes, traits, or abilities; moral or ethical strength; public estimation of someone; reputation."
[www.thefreedictionary.com]

If there is one thing that our world needs right now, it's character! Character is in critically short supply. Character anemia is the spiritual plague of our day. That's because character is more than just talkin' a good game; it's walkin' a good game. *Character consists of actions that back up the yap.* You can have talent, you can have gifts and abilities, you can be incredibly blessed and have all the money in the world, and yet still have no character.

Character is a choice by which you do what is right, instead of what brings you less pain or more gain.

You can never rise above the limitations of your character. If there are flaws in your character, then you will find yourself living right below the water line of that character problem. Success without a good foundation of character is bound for eventual failure.

Character Is as Character Does

How do you know when you've met somebody with character? You will find yourself saying things like this about them:

- I'd trust him with my life.
- You can always count on her.
- He keeps his word.
- She sure works hard.
- He will never take advantage of you.

- She is fair in all her dealings.
- If he said he would do it, then it's as good as done.
- She really cares about me. It's not just words.
- He radiates the love of Jesus
- She loves people.
- He is such a humble person.
- She is quick to admit when she is wrong.
- He is teachable.
- She is always honest with me.
- He is so much fun to be around.
- I trust her, even with my money.

If you're like me, reading that list makes me realize I have a lot more work to do on my character! Building character is a life-long project.

Cultural historian Warren Susman researched the rise and fall of the concept of character in his book, *Personality and the Making of Twentieth Century Culture*. During the 1800s, Warren claims that character was a key word in the vocabulary of both Brits and Americans. People were spoken of as having strong or weak character, good or bad character, a great deal of character or no character at all. Young people were encouraged to cultivate strong character, excellent character, and noble character and told that the most priceless achievement they could attain was to have "good character."

Susman's fascinating analysis continues into our modern-day cultural shift from *producing* to *consuming* and shows how the idea of what constitutes the *self* has shifted along with this cultural transformation. People no longer define themselves by their cultivation of virtue. Instead, their hobbies, dress, and material possessions became the new means of defining and expressing the self. In other words, *character went out of style.* Or as I would say, character became all *about* style!

How a Christ-follower handles the difficulties and the victories of his or her life will tell you a lot about the person's character. When things go incredibly well—you come into some serious money, for instance—a lot about your character comes to the surface. Do you run down to your church with a big tithe check to bless the work of the Lord, or do you race over to the Cadillac dealer to pick up a new Escalade? On the other end of the spectrum, a crisis doesn't always cultivate a stronger character, but it often reveals character flaws and weaknesses.

Difficult circumstances in our lives bring us to a crossroads where we must make a choice between the road to *character* or the shortcut to *compromise.*

Jesus demonstrated the ultimate example of flawless character, and every time we choose character over compromise, we grow more like Him.

Many people define character with this statement: "Character is who you are when no one is looking." It's not a bad idea, and in a way it applies to a little-known disciple named Jude— except that he was the subject of a great song by Paul McCartney of the Beatles called, "Hey Jude" (I'll bet you didn't know the Beatles are in the Bible—not). Seriously, Jude wrote a short *book* by the same name, and the whole focus of his little book is about *character*. You can just feel it when you read these verses:

> But, dear friends, remember what the apostles of
> our Lord Jesus Christ foretold. They said to you,
> "In the last times there will be scoffers who will
> follow their own ungodly desires." These are the
> people who divide you, who follow mere natural
> instincts and do not have the Spirit. (Jude 17-19)

Jude gets the credit for issuing a warning against loss of character. But he ends his short book (placed right before the book of Revelation in the New Testament) with one of the most beautiful dedications to Jesus ever written:

> To him who is able to keep you from stumbling
> and to present you before his glorious presence
> without fault and with great joy—to the only God
> our Savior be glory, majesty, power and authority,
> through Jesus Christ our Lord, before all ages,
> now and forevermore! Amen. (Jude 24-25)

In other words, Jude says Jesus can build our character to the point where we will stop stumbling and walk in complete integrity.

Little Boy, Big Character

The first person I think of when I think of character is my ten-year-old son, Josiah. We named him after King Josiah in the Bible. He was an eight-year-old king who reigned for thirty-one years. Second Kings 22:2 summarizes his life by saying that King Josiah "did what was right in the eyes of the Lord." That's what true character is all about—doing right in the eyes of the Lord—and that's my son, Josiah. He is a special young man who lives with a deep desire to please the Lord. I often find him reading the Bible, alone in his bedroom, for hours on end.

One day at school, a couple of his classmates got into trouble for talking and had their lights moved (the teacher's negative reward of choice). At that, Josiah went up to the teacher and said, "You should move my light too because I was also talking." That's Josiah. He doesn't always do the right thing, but he does the right thing even when he's done the wrong thing. If there was ever a person whom I thought was the closest to Christ's character, it would be Josiah. I feel like I learn more from him than he will ever learn from me.

Josiah's character shows through his loving, compassionate, and kind heart. One Christmas morning, for example, Josiah excitedly brought me a present he had wrapped all by himself. As I opened the box, there sat a baseball and football of his that he decided to wrap and give to his dad.

Then there's the story of "twin day" at his school. He and his buddy were planning what to wear as look-alikes, and a third kid—the kid who always seemed to get left out of everything—came up to Josiah and his buddy and asked if he could join them. They could be triplets. Josiah's buddy quickly complained that it was *twin*, not triplet, day. As the three boys parted ways, though, Josiah whispered to the lonely boy what he and his friend were planning to wear so the boy could match them.

Big Men, Big Character

While I realize every parent sees through "parent lenses" when it comes to their kids, I do believe Josiah's character is the real deal. But another person also comes to mind when I think of character: my good friend, Jake Voskuhl. Jake and I became friends when I first became team chaplain for the Suns back in 2002.

Jake played nine years in the NBA but before he went pro, Jake was a 1999 NCAA National Champion at UCONN. He possesses a great deal of skill (and height!), but more than that, he has character. Jake never missed an NBA chapel service, and I mean *never*. Not only was Jake faithful to chapel, he was faithful to Jesus. And, to be clear, there's a big difference! Many players who are faithful to attend chapel are not at all faithful to Christ. Let's face it: we all have the tendency to show up at church every Sunday but completely leave Jesus in the church building when we walk out. That's because it's easier to faithfully attend church and skip the faithful-to-Jesus part than to remain faithful to Jesus and skip the church attendance part.

Many people who boldly claim Christ on Sundays are boldly ashamed of Christ come Monday.

Jake loved the Lord, loved his family, loved people, and was a true man of character. Over the years, the Voskuhls and the Hearns became great family friends. We took vacations together, celebrated holidays together, and spent days boating and jet skiing.

Early in his career, I remember watching how he would position himself during team huddles. He stood with his back to the court and his face toward the bench. One day, I asked him why he did this since I could tell he did it on purpose. He said, "I like to keep my face to the bench because that's where my coach is and keep my back to the court because that's where the dancers are." Wow! How awesome is that? That is truly Jake. He strives at all times and in every situation to be a man of character. Jake always makes sure he focuses on the right things, and he keeps the wrong things out of his sight. It doesn't even matter to Jake whether or not anyone notices what he's doing. He does what is right, no matter what.

Like Jake, the best way you can find the right focus for your life is to cultivate your character. You have only to watch or read the news for a few minutes before you realize that most of the scandals and problems and difficulties we face in our lives, our country, and our world have to do with a lack of character. We could use a bit more character, couldn't we?

Being a person of character means doing the right thing—the God-thing—even when the wrong thing or the selfish thing looks enticing. And being a person of character won't always be the easy route, and it won't always provide the most self-gratifying path.

I'll never forget my first year serving as team chaplain for the Kansas City Royals baseball team. During spring training 2002, major league all-star slugger, Mike Sweeney, and now San Francisco Giants pitcher Jeremy Affeldt (two more men of character) invited me to breakfast.

As we were finishing our meals, Mike said to me, "Travis, we have really appreciated having you be our pastor and our chaplain this spring training, and Jeremy and I want to give you a tithe." I nearly spit my eggs across the table! This is the thought that raced through my mind: *Sweeney alone made $12 million bucks this year! If he tithed two months from spring training to me, that'd be $200 grand!* (See, I'm human.) But—thank God—that's not what I said. I responded with, "No way, guys. No way. I really appreciate the kind thought, but I'm not here for your money. I'm here to serve you. I am gainfully employed and besides the biblical model for tithing is that you tithe to the church you attend." Mike responded, "Yes, but *you* have been our church for the last two months!" (Oh devil, go away!) I said, "No, Mike, I'm not your church, and I'm not taking your money! You need to tithe to wherever you call your home church and your regular place of worship."

I've had many of losses in my life, but that was a huge victory—a victory for character. I managed to do the right thing, the God-thing, even when the wrong, selfish thing would have benefited me greatly!

Responsible Character

I'm clearly not the sharpest crayon in the box. But I do strive for integrity and character. In part, I know it is what God expects of me, but I also understand that I have influence. We all do. God has not only given me the responsibility to influence my family and my church but also to "influence the influencers."

In all those years of playing the game of life for myself, I had no idea God was going to use it all for His glory and His mission. After growing up with a ball constantly in my hands, I can now see that God was developing in me an appreciation for sports and compassion for pro athletes. God gave me a love for sports so that one day I would be able to influence the influencers *for Him*. It's weird that athletes have so much influence in our culture—especially with our children, teenagers, and young adults. With such a huge influence comes huge responsibility, but consider what Charles Barkley says of himself: "I ain't no role model."

Wrong-o, Chuck. You are, in fact, a role model whether you want to be or not. Barkley is still a huge influencer *and* role model, even years after retiring from the NBA. The same is true of many other pro athletes. Some celebrities try to duck out of being an influencer, without realizing they have major impact , regardless of whether they asked for it or not. In our interconnected culture, the world is a stage, and people with talent have sway over millions.

I've seen this time and time again. At Impact Church, we've invited some of the biggest names in music, entertainment, television, or pop culture to be our special guests, but the biggest crowds *always* come when there's a professional athlete in the house. For some reason, people are especially intrigued by athletes. Their fame, the discipline required to achieve their level of performance, the money they make, the lifestyles they live—all stimulate immense curiosity from young and old alike. That also creates a platform which can be used to greatly benefit any cause or campaign an athlete adopts and makes his or her own. That is why I have always had a heart to "influence the influencers."

I planned to interview Phoenix Suns player, Josh Childress, at church one Sunday, and when he tweeted that he was going to be speaking at his home church, more people than we could count showed up just to see him. One person who came that Sunday was the Arizona Diamondbacks mascot, a good buddy of mine, who became a Christian that very day! He showed up because of Josh Childress' tweet—and got saved because of the influence of Josh's character.

The Bible tells us about a man during the time of Jesus who was a great influencer. He was a centurion, a leader in charge of a detachment of soldiers. The story takes ten verses to tell, but it is worth every word! Take a look at Luke 7:1-10:

> When Jesus had finished saying all this in the
> hearing of the people, he entered Capernaum.
> There a centurion's servant, whom his master
> valued highly, was sick and about to die. The
> centurion heard of Jesus and sent some elders
> of the Jews to him, asking him to come and
> heal his servant. When they came to Jesus, they
> pleaded earnestly with him, "This man deserves
> to have you do this, because he loves our nation
> and has built our synagogue." So Jesus went with
> them. He was not far from the house when the
> centurion sent friends to say to him: "Lord, don't
> trouble yourself, for I do not deserve to have you
> come under my roof. That is why I did not even
> consider myself worthy to come to you. But say
> the word, and my servant will be healed. For I
> myself am a man under authority, with soldiers
> under me. I tell this one, 'Go,' and he goes; and

that one, 'Come,' and he comes. I say to my
servant, 'Do this,' and he does it.'" When Jesus
heard this, he was amazed at him, and turning
to the crowd following him, he said, "I tell you,
I have not found such great faith even in Israel."
Then the men who had been sent returned to the
house and found the servant well.

You may have read that story many times before, but I want
to point out two things that should be turbo-charging off the
page at you. The first is this: the centurion was full of character.
How awesome must this guy have been that his friends would
go to Jesus and say, "This guy *deserves* to have you do this!" Do
you have friends like that? They gave a character reference to
Jesus on the spot. They explained, "He's involved in all kinds of
great projects that help other people." What a testimony! This
man had made a lasting impression on the whole town. Everybody who knew him loved him. That's the kind of person I want
to be—somebody that *other* people speak highly of.

The second thing that jumps off the page is this: he was
a huge influencer. In fact, he understood that all of us have
the power to influence others and also have a responsibility
to carefully pick who is going to influence us. This centurion
said, "Jesus, I believe in you, and I understand your power and
authority over me." That was such a radical statement of humility and character, Jesus responded, "You know what, I haven't
found such great *faith* in all of Israel!"

There is something contagious about people of great character. If you want to see miracles happen in your life, just like
the centurion, start letting God cultivate a spiritual depth in

your character. Grow your faith in Jesus Christ, and watch how life starts to change. You, too, can be an influencer wherever God places you.

Whenever I walk into the arena in downtown Phoenix, I picture it as a massive church that seats nineteen thousand people. There are security guards, players, spectators, concession stand operators, cheerleaders, camera operators, ticket handlers, referees, and a host of other people there, all focused on producing an exciting basketball game that all of us want to watch. But behind every face, there is a drama unfolding. Everyone has a hidden hurt. The players are no different than all the other people in the arena. The whole set-up is one big chapel, and everyone needs a healer for their hidden hurts. *Everybody there needs Jesus.*

Each person has struggles and difficulties, broken relationships or financial challenges, family drama or health problems. In order to minister effectively to such a diverse group, the key is not to have all the talent in the world or all the answers or to be the best counselor or problem solver. As Theodore Roosevelt said, "No one cares how much you know until they know how much you care." I'm convinced no one cares if I know much of anything, but they do care if I care. And to care like Jesus cares boils down to one thing—*having character*. People can see a fake coming from a mile away. Real recognizes real, and God wants all of us to be people of real character.

Being a person of character is game-changing.

As all-star defensive linebacker, Ray Lewis, of the Baltimore Ravens said, "Don't walk through life just [*insert whatever you're currently doing with your life*]. Character and integrity and really making an impact on someone's life. That's the ultimate vision; that's the ultimate goal—bottom line."

You are a game changer, so be a person of character! I hope reading this chapter has ignited something deep within your spirit. Maybe you have been caught napping when it comes to character development. Maybe you have been more worried about your appearances and your reputation than about your character, and you've realized that you've wasted time with that. I hope you are rising up in holy, righteous excitement. From this day forward and for the rest of your life, you are going to be a character machine! You are going to watch for ways to develop your character. You are going to be a person of strong character, a person who values character above all else. When people think of you, they are going to start saying things like, "I trust you with my life" and "I have never met a person with more character."

Make a vow that you will let Jesus develop the sweetest character in you. You'll pour over your Bible, get callouses on your knees from praying, and you'll sing even if it sounds terrible, because you can't let a day go by without busting out in worship to the Lord. You will take the high road and never the low road. You would rather go through pain, than lie about anything. You would rather know you have done the right thing, than the easy thing. You are never going to be the same. Character just became one of your primary objectives in life!

Prayer for Character

Dear Jesus,

There is only one thing I can take to heaven with me: my character. I can't take possessions. I can't take any money. I can't even take my friends. But I can take my character. So, Lord, I pray that I will become more aware of developing my character. Help me find opportunities every day where I will have a choice to take the road less traveled, and develop my character, or to take the easy road, and compromise. Help me to be alert to those moments and to pick the right direction when they come. Help me be somebody that everybody knows as a person of strong character.

In Jesus Name. Amen.

Scriptures to Reflect on

Colossians 3:12-15
Galatians 5:16-17
Psalm 127:1

Chapter 10

MULTIPLY

"Do not let what you cannot do interfere with
what you can do."

—John Wooden, College Basketball Hall
of Fame player and coach

Featured Disciple:
Judas Iscariot, the disciple who betrayed Jesus, who didn't trust
Him to multiply what they had to meet their needs.

---

*"But the word of the Lord continued to grow and to
be multiplied."*
Acts 12:24

Multiply is "to increase or cause to increase the amount, number,
or degree of; to grow in amount, number, or degree"
[www.thefreedictionary.com]

God loves to take the simplest, smallest thing you have to offer and *multiply* it way farther than you could ever imagine. I'll share a lot in this chapter about what God will do if you trust Him to multiply your blessings, but first, let's talk about the contrast that happens if you don't.

Spiritual Subtraction

There is only *one verse* prior to the Last Supper in which any words of the disciple Judas Iscariot are recorded. The passage, John 12:4-6, offers a great deal of insight, though, into this man's character:

> But one of his disciples, Judas Iscariot, who was later to betray him, objected, "Why wasn't this perfume sold and the money given to the poor? It was worth a year's wages." He did not say this because he cared about the poor but because he was a thief; as keeper of the money bag, he used to help himself to what was put into it.

A lot of people think Judas was probably never saved. Maybe they're right, but if you read the Gospel accounts, it sure seems to say Judas was sent out and empowered, just like the other eleven disciples. Scripture says Jesus sent the *twelve* to cast out demons and heal people. Judas would have been among them. He was certainly in the boat during the storm Jesus calmed. He saw Peter walk on water. I think Judas was the real deal, but . . . he had a weakness, one that he never got help with.

When Judas first felt tempted by the money, right then he should have gone to Jesus and said, "Keeping this money thing in line is too much of a struggle for me. Give the bag to somebody else." But because he didn't, look what happened! *Money* got a tighter and tighter grip on Judas until he eventually imagined, *Dude, if I can just get thirty pieces of silver, I'll be rich!* Historians have estimated that thirty pieces of silver in Jesus' day was worth enough to purchase an entire farm—perhaps as much as a quarter of a million dollars! That's some very serious cash.

Judas' problem grew over time. Little by little, he fudged with the money bag. Then when big-temptation day came along, he couldn't handle it and fell hard.

But yeah, I get it. Maybe Judas never *was* saved . . . and I'm sure you and I have never put money or possessions ahead of our relationship with Christ either, right? I often tease the folks in my church not to use their tithe money for a car payment or thirty lattes at Starbucks. But maybe that's not so funny.

You have to learn to trust God to *multiply* what you have.

The money bag. It's one of Satan's best tricks. Start small, just a little compromise. No big deal. But the small concessions numb your soul so that when the big temptation stares you in the face, you don't even recognize the danger. You've been set up for a fall. So how do you sidestep this terrible possibility?

The bottom line with Judas is that he didn't trust Jesus to multiply what little he had and make it go far enough. Instead, Judas thought he had to steal from the money bag and look for other ways to gather funds, because he worried that Jesus wouldn't make sure that what he had was enough. Judas' main issue was *trust*.

Key Factors in Multiplying

My life consists of one story after another of God doing way more than I could ever imagine, and He usually chooses to do it with ridiculously small starts. On the surface, most of my stories start as no big deal, but then God kicks in with his multiplication miracle, and amazing things happen. I can hardly comprehend how it happens, over and over again. God loves to take humble beginnings and multiply them into a result that takes our breath away.

I once launched a youth group in a start-up church that met at an elementary school. We didn't even have a room of our own. We met in the hallway. Oh, and one other thing: the building had no air conditioning—in Phoenix, Arizona! Believe me. No A/C plus fifty or sixty teenagers crammed together equals much bad smell. I led the band and worship singers with sweat flowing like Niagara Falls down my face.

Years later, when our youth group had grown to more than seven hundred kids, people often asked, "How did you grow your youth group to be so big?" I could only laugh in amazement as I explained what God started in a stinky school hallway with no air conditioning.

From small starts, the Bible talks about how God sets the stage for great things to happen, and it begins with people walking in "humble beginnings." I love this verse Micah 6:8:

> He has shown you, O mortal, what is good. And
> what does the Lord require of you? To act justly
> and to love mercy and to walk humbly with your
> God.

In my second season with the Royals, Garth Brooks "joined" the team. He was doing publicity to raise money for a worthwhile foundation, and in the process, he and I became good friends. He attended our chapel service at the Royals clubhouse, but his presence gave me pause. You see, I always brought my guitar so I could start the service with a few songs. Talk about intimidating! So when Garth was there early on I simply handed him my guitar and said, "Man, they want you to play, not me!" He just smiled and responded, "That's really nice of you to say, but I think you do a fine job." So there I was, playing my really bad guitar and singing probably even worse, with Garth Brooks in my audience! It really didn't seem to matter to Garth, though. He sat there, smiling, clapping, and singing praise to the Lord, right along with everyone else.

During that same season, Mike Sweeney came on as the Royals' franchise player, and in spite of his $12-million-a-year contract, he was one of the most down-to-earth, godly men I have ever met. Once after chapel, he came up to me with these especially exciting words: "Hey, Trav, during chapel, your message gave another guy enough courage that he finally took the step, and got saved, and gave his life to Jesus. And I wanted you to know, that it was because of your message!"

It was beyond cool to think that my minor league efforts at giving the players a meaningful chapel service were working. Somebody got saved in a locker room, accompanied by my amateur guitar playing, bad singing, and sorry preaching. How cool! God knows how to multiply what we offer, which means we just need to keep on going.

"Opportunities multiply as they are seized."
—Sun Tzu

To this day, I know all these miracles happened because of the favor God gave me and the incredible way in which God put things together. His favor took another leap forward in 2004 as I took another small step.

All Rapped Up

I told (my) Natalie that it's amazing how God can take a little thought, one little idea, and turn it into something massive, and during the 2004 Royals spring training season, I told Natalie my next little idea. I said was going to write a song for the Royals.

"I think it's gonna be like a hot combination of a hip-hop and rock song," I explained. I had in mind big beats and big guitars. I pictured that, when the players arrived for spring training, I would hand out a bunch of CDs of the song to the players (these were the days before iTunes).

My only goal was to inspire these ballplayers to have a great season. I wanted them to know that I was rootin' for them, and I figured it was part of my job as a chaplain to encourage these guys to *go after it.*

So, I wrote a song and recorded it. The piece sounded okay, but it was certainly nothing amazing. Still, it was a song, and it was a song for *the team.* The Royals' theme for that year was "Together we can," so that's what I named the song, "Together We Can." I also came up with a crazy idea of how to change the song up. I created a hook that was a crowd-type chant for the chorus, and I wrote hip-hop lyrics that included every player on the roster by name. I wanted the verses to really build each of them up. It was a major challenge to work in all the player names! I also had to find out what they were known for on the field, and how to work their cool athletic attributes into the song. When I finally had the whole song figured out, I got really excited.

With the help of a few friends to do the band tracks, I got the CD recorded in a studio, including some killer vocals (me among them, of course). After the recording was done, I took my one copy to the locker room and told Mike Sweeney, "Swee-nDawg, you gotta listen to this, just for a second. I think you'll like it."

I just wanted to see what his thoughts were, so he took the unlabeled CD and stuck it in a little bootleg CD player he kept in his locker. As the first verse played, he started to get excited, (maybe because the first verse is about him), and he says, "Man,

Travis, I didn't know what you were talking about. This is amazing! I can't believe you did this!"

The next thing I know, he'd called all the guys to the weight room where the sound system is killer. He pushed "play," the song hit, and every guy in the room lit up. Thirty players started circling the weight room sound system, and they were buzzin'! That's when I knew I was onto something.

The team—and as a result, my song—included some great baseball players: Mike Sweeney and Jeremy Affeldt, Carlos Beltran and DJ Carrasco, Jason Grimsley and Joe Randa, to name just a few.

The next day, a reporter called me from the *Kansas City Star*. The man on the phone said, "Hey, Travis, I heard you wrote the new theme song for the Kansas City Royals. I was just wondering if I can interview you and do a story on this."

I was shocked. *I* wrote the new theme song?

"You've got to be kidding me," I told him." This is crazy!" But he wasn't kidding at all. He drove out to the locker room at the spring training stadium to interview me.

For the interview, he stuck a microphone in my face and scribbled at light speed on a notepad. Although I answered his questions, I was way intimidated. But players who walked by while I was talking to the reporter high-fived me. It was bizarre. I wasn't ready for what was happening.

After a series of questions, the reporter concluded, "Let me ask you: where can all of Kansas City get a copy of this song?"

Whoa! I'm thinking: *I have no copyright, and I've only got one copy of the song.* So I said, "You know what? They can go to radiantsports.com."

I made up that domain name on the spot, hoping it was available (that was before everybody was scooping up domain names right and left). Doing stuff like this is what I call, "1-800-wingin'-it"!

So half my brain is yelling at me that I don't even have a copyright for this song, only have one copy, and no real website. The other half is saying, "Go for it, dude, and see what God does with this!"

Then the reporter asked, "How much are they?"

I did some real quick thinking: it's a theme song at the stadium, where even the hot dogs cost nine dollars a piece, so this can't be too cheap. "Eight dollars!" I exploded.

I realize that in today's world of iTunes, asking eight bucks for one song sounds absurd, but at the time, you couldn't buy a song for just a dollar. And it was a theme song, right?

The interview took maybe twenty minutes, and afterward, he told me, "This is going to be an overnight sensation—a big hit—so I'm going to have this ready for tomorrow's newspaper."

And was it ever! The next day, his story hit the *Kansas City Star* with a front page headline!

The interview left me stunned, but I jumped in my car and called a buddy of mine I knew could help me. "Dude," I said, "who builds websites? I need you to tell me right now, like *right now*! I need you to look—right now!—and see if radiantsports. com is available."

While we talked, he checked online, and miraculously, the URL was available! So I went on, "Dude, listen, I need you to build me a page *today*—just one page—and I need a CD cover! I just took a picture in the locker room of Mike Sweeney, Carlos

Beltran, Jeremy Affeldt, and me. I need you to turn it into a CD cover and title it 'Together We Can!' And I need every bit of this overnight—all of it on the website by tomorrow!"

At first there was silence on the other end of the phone. Then he said simply, "Are you kidding me?"

An artist, this is a guy who does not like pressure but pulled the all-nighter of all-nighters and got the CD designed, website built, and all of it online while I started cranking out copies of the CD.

Sure enough, the next day's front page shouted, "Listen to the Royals Rap Song" and "Royals Chaplain Raps Out a Hit"!

Instantly, I had a new nickname: The Rappin' Chaplain. From there, the scenario mushroomed. Buddies of mine from all over Kansas City started sending me texts like, "Trav! Just heard your song on the radio!"

My interview made it onto the radio, and a total stranger from Kansas City called me and said, "Hey man, we just saw your article in the newspaper. We're a reproduction company and can print a thousand copies of those CD's. I want to propose something to you. How about we print, bar code, and shrink wrap fifteen thousand for free, and you can donate them to whatever cause you would like for the Kansas City Royals?"

Since the song included the players' names, there were a bunch of charities that wanted to sell the CDs as a fund raiser. This got the attention of the players' wives who loved the charity angle. Everything was getting crazier by the minute!

Then, just when I thought it couldn't get any more ridiculous, my phone rang, and the voice on the other end of the line said, "Travis, this is Dan Glass of the Kansas City Royals." The *owner*! And not just of the Royals—he owns several Wal Marts, to boot. "I need to speak with you in my office," he announced.

Uh oh, maybe I'm in trouble for "writing the Royals theme song," even though it was an accident! I couldn't sleep that night. I spent most of the time praying, "Please, God, please just let it be okay! You know I'm trying to do this for you, Lord. Give me favor!"

At my meeting the next day with Mr. Glass, he got straight to the point. "I understand you wrote the theme song for our baseball team this year?"

It sounded like a loaded question to me, so I said, "Well, I wrote a song to inspire the guys. Music is a big motivator, and I was just trying inspire the team."

"Yes. That's great!" he responded, "I've heard the song. I saw the article." (I thought it was funny that the owner of the ball team had to read about it in the paper, but I didn't think it was a good time to laugh.) He continued, "Travis, I had a thought: what would you think about selling them in the stadium?"

"It's funny you should ask, because I was just approached by someone who wants to make fifteen thousand copies. So I think that's a great idea, Mr. Glass."

His enthusiasm grew. "Great! We can put them in the team shops. The other thought I had was that we do something every year called faith and family night, and we average about thirty-five thousand people at that game. This year, Mike Sweeney and Jeremy Affeldt will be giving their testimonies, and we think it would be cool—if you're up for it—for you to open by performing your song live." (In front of thirty-five thousand people!)

Whaaaaaaat? I could hardly answer him fast enough: "Um, let me pray about that—yes! Absolutely! I would love the chance to perform the song live in front of thirty-five thousand people!" But I was thinking to myself, *This is crazy, crazy, crazy! I've never performed in front of one thousand people, much less thirty-five thousand!* I was freaking out!

Mr. Glass told me the team would pay for the flight, room, and other travel expenses for Natalie and me to go there for a week, just hang out, and go to the games. I remember thinking, *what an amazing thing when God starts to multiply the little bit you have!* If you simply try and make it a point to give everything you have, God makes more of your efforts than you could have ever created on your own.

God continually shows us that He loves to take humble beginnings and multiply them into miracles that you could never imagine in a thousand years.

The Bible reminds us about how this multiplication miracle works:

> His master replied, "Well done, good and faithful servant! You have been faithful with a few things; I will put you in charge of many things. Come and share your master's happiness!" (Matthew 25:23)

Faithfulness in the small things is what releases the multiplication blessing into your life. God watches you with the small stuff!

Catch and Release—to God

There's a great story in the Bible of God multiplying the very little somebody had into a miraculous experience for thousands. I like to call it the story of "the Happy Meal that wouldn't end."

In one of Jesus' amazing teaching sessions, time seemed to stand still. Nobody noticed the day slipping away, and before they knew it, dinner hour was upon them. As the sun started to slip toward the horizon, the twelve disciples realized there were no places to buy food, because they were in a remote area. When they checked to see if people had brought food with them, all they came up with was a boy who had five loaves of bread and two fish, the equivalent of a first-century happy meal.

When the disciples pointed out that the resources were way too small to accomplish a sit down dinner for five thousand, Jesus was undeterred. "Have them sit down," He said. Then He lifted up those measly loaves and fishes, gave thanks to God for them, and started passing them out to the people. And check out how Jesus *multiplied* the boy's little bit of food:

> [Jesus] broke the loaves. Then he gave them to his disciples to set before the people. He also divided the two fish among them all. They all ate and were satisfied. (Mark 6:41b-42)

Notice, too, that the scripture doesn't say, "Everybody got a little bit to eat, to tide them over until they could get back home and enjoy a good home-cooked meal." Nope. It says, "They ate and *were satisfied.*" They ate like ravenous wolves. They *chowed down.* They killed it!

And just so we don't miss the inconceivable multiplication that Jesus caused, there is a remarkable footnote to the story about the leftovers, where at first, it seemed like there wouldn't be enough: "And the disciples picked up twelve basketfuls of broken pieces of bread and fish" (Mark 6:43).

What's more, I don't think it's a coincidence that there were exactly *twelve* baskets of leftovers. I think it was meant for each disciple to have one.

I suspect that, as they were picking up the leftover food, there came a moment when each disciple was holding a basket full of food. And they probably each came walking back over to Jesus, holding a basket. I'll bet Jesus just looked at them, smiled, and probably said something like, "Andrew, had a little left over, huh? Philip, that looks heavy; you got that? Hey, Peter, you got a basket too; good for you! Wow, boys, look at that: exactly twelve baskets of leftovers. What a coincidence!" Every one of the disciples learned something that day. Jesus made sure each one got to hold a basket full of multiplication.

The Bible is extremely clear that your entire life is about multiplication. In the Old Testament, one of my favorite verses offers a cool picture of how God multiplies, without ever saying the word itself. Check out Ecclesiastes 11:1: "Cast your bread upon the waters, for you will find it after many days" (ESV).

Life isn't about the multiplication of all you accumulate; it's about the multiplication of all you release back to God.

At one time when I read this verse, I pictured feeding the ducks on a pond by our first house. Those ducks raced like Olympians over to where anybody was throwing pieces of stale bread into the water. And it's not such a bad comparison. Ecclesiastes 11:1 is a beautiful verse about *releasing* in order to *multiply*.

But here's another analogy. Centuries ago, American merchants sent off their goods back to the old world on ships. In those days—before wire transfers, electronic banking, and overnight shipping—you had to have faith that the goods you sent were going to come back to you in the form of payment. You had to release what you worked hard to achieve in order to see it multiplied, to see it come back in the form of profit. Back then, when you "cast your bread upon the waters," there was no guarantee, no sure thing. It was a step of faith because there was no telling if the reward would ever come back to you.

Once that merchant ship set sail and your "bread" was on board, anything could happen. Pirates could board the ship and rob the vessel of its cargo. The ship could be lost at sea or run aground on a reef or be smashed to bits in a ferocious storm. Similarly, when you *cast your bread upon the waters*, you are *trusting* that your bread will make it to the market and bring you back a bigger profit than you ever imagined!

Sometimes we hesitate to put our faith completely in the Lord for multiplication. Sometimes we just sit on the shore of faith, holding tightly to our little pieces of bread, and giving thanks for it, rather than casting it upon the water so it can multiply. God tells us over and over in His word to *go for it*, to step out in the blessing of multiplication, and to watch what He will do.

When you leave behind the security of what you know, what you already have, and what you are sure of, that's when God can move, and He promises it will be a worthwhile investment. Luke 18:28-30 explains:

> Peter said to Jesus, "We have left all we had to follow you!" "Yes," said Jesus, "and you won't regret it. No one who has sacrificed home, spouse, brothers and sisters, parents, children— whatever—will lose out. It will all come back *multiplied* many times over in your lifetime. And then the bonus of eternal life!" (NIV and THE MESSAGE, emphasis mine)

Did you notice two key phrases there? One is "who has sacrificed," and the other is "multiplied many times." Jesus wasn't saying you had to give up your family, your kids, and your parents. He was merely emphasizing that, when we sacrifice something for Jesus, we will get blessings multiplied back to us *here on earth*. And to put the icing on the cake, we also get the bonus of eternal life!

You might be looking at your situation right now and thinking, "This just isn't going to work out. It doesn't add up!" And you know which word just doesn't cut it? The word *add*. God never seems to work with addition. He does multiplication! If you're doing the math like the disciples on that day when five thousand hungry people were staring at them on a grassy hillside, you might be tempted to lose hope because your prospects seem slim.

But, on the other hand, no, I guess you wouldn't. Not you. That's not gonna happen because . . . you guessed it: You are a game changer!

For the rest of your life, remember Micah 6:8. All God asks is for you to walk humbly with Him. That's what ignites multiplication.

I heard a great story about a hunter walking through the African jungle who found a huge dead warthog and a pygmy standing beside it. Amazed, he asked, "Did you kill that warthog?"

"Yes," the pygmy answered.

"How could a little guy like you kill a huge beast like that?" wondered the hunter.

"I killed it with my club," the pygmy claimed.

The astonished hunter asked, "How big is your club?"

"There's about sixty of us," the pygmy explained.

His final answer probably wasn't what you were expecting, was it? That's because we don't naturally think of multiplication. We think of addition—of one person, of our limitations, of the "hugeness" of the problem. We forget we have a "club" when we unite our hearts and efforts with Jesus to overcome the problem, solve the dilemma, or handle the issue.

Instead of trying to figure out how to solve things yourself, just relax in the assurance that you are walking with Him. If God is by your side, taking a stroll with you, how could your path be the wrong one? Multiplication will come naturally.

That's how God works. You just need to believe, have faith, and trust His provision!

You are now going to become an expert at looking for God's multiplication factor. You are going to look at every scenario expectantly, hoping to see yet another time when God multiplies your efforts to produce an exciting miracle.

Prayer for Multiplication

Dear Jesus,

I have a natural tendency to be just like Judas Iscariot and to worry that I won't have enough. As ridiculous as it sounds, I am afraid to trust You to meet all my needs, even though You have the power to multiply even the smallest of efforts. Lord, I trust You but need help in those areas where I am challenged to trust You *completely*! I turn all of my worries over to You, right now. I am going to let go of whatever keeps me clinging to things that offer no real security. I am going to be on the lookout for small opportunities because that is where You typically work a miracle of multiplication. Keep me faithful in small things, so I can see You use me for even greater things.

In Jesus Name. Amen.

Scriptures to Reflect on

Matthew 13:23
Acts 2:47
Jeremiah 30:19

Chapter 11

INFLUENCE

"For many, my behavior has been a major disappointment, my behavior has caused considerable worry to my business partners, and everyone involved in my business, but most importantly to the young people we influence, I apologize."

—TIGER WOODS, PROFESSIONAL GOLFING LEGEND

Featured Disciple:
Philip, the disciple who missed an opportunity to influence others.

"The Jews received Paul's message with enthusiasm and met with him daily, examining the Scriptures to see if they supported what he said. A lot of them became believers, including many Greeks who were prominent in the community, women and men of influence."
Acts 17:11-12 (THE MESSAGE)

Influence is "a power affecting a person, thing, or course of events, especially one that operates without any direct or apparent effort; Power to sway or affect based on prestige, wealth, ability, or position."
[www.thefreedictionary.com]

I believe many of us underestimate the power of influence. We miss incredible opportunities all around us to influence people, to change a situation, to make the world a better place, and to be champions for creative new solutions to lots of really old problems.

Your life is one humongous opportunity to influence the people around you and to change the course of history.

We need more influencers in this world, people who will step up to the plate and keep swinging, even when they miss or strike out. We need more people who walk with their heads held high, their determined faces turned to the wind, who will take great strides and make bold moves to do something great in this world. But we don't always make the most of our opportunities of influence.

God-Sized Influence

If there was ever a person who missed an opportunity to influence the people around him, it was the disciple, Philip. When Jesus had been teaching five thousand people all day and the sun was starting to set, Philip saw lots of people looking at him with hunger in their eyes and had an opportunity to be an influencer, but he missed it. Check out John 6:5-6 to see how this story unfolded:

> When Jesus looked up and saw a great crowd
> coming toward him, he said to Philip, "Where
> shall we buy bread for these people to eat?" He
> asked this only to test him, for he already had in
> mind what he was going to do.

Notice that Jesus is being almost comical here, messing with Philip. Can't you just picture the scene? The crowd was probably around twenty thousand if you include women and children along with the men. The disciples had given up their jobs to follow Jesus, and they're broke. You'll recall that Judas Iscariot carried around the money bag, so that means that it only took *one* money bag to hold all the money that all twelve disciples plus Jesus had! I'm pretty sure there was a "shortage of fundage," as we say.

And Jesus (you gotta love this) turns to Philip and says, "Where shall we buy bread for these people to eat?"

Why in the world would He ask such a nutty question? Suppose I met you at the US Airways center when it was full of people watching a ball game and said, "Where can we buy some food for these twenty thousand people?" What would you say to me? You'd probably laugh. You certainly wouldn't take me seriously. But remember *who* was asking Philip: Jesus! Scripture says *"he asked this only to test him."* Jesus was fishing for something with Philip. He wanted to see if Philip would have the right reaction. It was a test. Notice that "Jesus already knew what he was going to do." He already had the answer in mind, but He wanted to know if *Philip* knew He had the answer.

It's the same for you and me. Whatever problem you're going through, God has the answer. He already knows the solution, but He might put something in your path where it seems *He* is asking *you*, "What should we do?" He wants to test you to see if you say, "Jesus, You, of course, have the answer."

Philip had a moment in time when he could have answered brilliantly and been *the* influencer of everyone who was watching that day. All the hungry eyes were on him when Jesus asked the question—and Philip blew it. And not just once with his initial response. He kept on blowing it. Look at what he said: "Philip answered him, 'Eight months' wages would not buy enough bread for each one to have a bite" (John 6:7).

Have you ever met somebody who likes to do things by the numbers? Usually it's an engineer, an accountant, or a banker. Apparently, Philip was a numbers guy too. His analytical mind kicked into gear, and he quickly did some calculating. His analysis went something like this: "Jesus, it would take someone's life savings to pull this off."

Philip is not exactly your "out of the box" thinker. He just does the math. "*Buy* the food? No way that's happening!"

If he would have thought—for even just one second—he might have answered correctly. He might have said, "What? Are you kidding, Jesus? Are you for real? *You're* the 'water into wine' guy! Dude, I know you can bust us out some rib-eye steaks with no problem! So here, let me just get everyone to sit down with their steak knives, and you can start whoopin' us up another miracle!"

But Philip couldn't get those numbers out of his head—and that made him *doubt*. His eyes were looking directly at the God of the impossible, but all his mind could see *was* the impossible.

When you look at the impossible, remember,
you have a big God! Jesus is bigger than any
problem you've got.

Reading in the Bible about the miracles of Jesus, you'll discover this: He loved to go *way* past the minimum requirement. The blind person He healed could see *20/20*, not just a little bit, when Jesus was done. When he healed a guy who couldn't walk, he left *dancing*! Jesus picked out the town *prostitute* and turned her into a *devoted* believer! We should set our expectations so high that God will far surpass the minimum requirement. You should be expecting a feast, not just a snack to take the edge off your hunger! When you have that kind of expectation about the miracles God can do, it turns you into a powerful influencer for Him.

Over *All* Influence

Growing up in a small town in tough family circumstances like I did, you really start to wonder whether you will ever make a mark for Christ on this world. It was easy for me to figure that I was just going to be an average guy and spend all my days just trying to get ahead and make a life for myself. I didn't think I would ever be somebody who had the opportunity to influence people, and I certainly never dreamed I would be somebody who would "influence the influencers." What I have come to find out, though, is this: everybody and anybody can become an influencer of influencers if you change the way you look at your life.

It is easy to fall into the trap of thinking you have no influence on your circumstances, the people around you, or your dreams for the future. Maybe you've even spoken words of defeat, giving up before you ever get started. People call that "the victim mentality," where you view everything that happens to you as something you cannot influence or control. Yes, things happen that are out of your control. Only a total idiot would say that you can control life, because you definitely cannot control the crazy things that come at you out of nowhere. But there are many things that you *can* control and *influence*. I want to see you bust out of a defeated mentality and take on a whole new level of influence with your life!

In the last few years, I have seen influence in a way different light than before. Having had the chance to meet people with huge amounts of influence, I now believe influence is another major game changer.

If you are going to be a game changer, you must be a person of influence with your family, your church, your city, and the world.

My work as a chaplain to professional athletes is a volunteer job, with no official recognition and no built-in authority or power to go with it. But you know what? Being a chaplain in my situation is truly the definition of a position of influence.

During my first year with the Phoenix Suns, I have to admit, I was star-struck. Sure, I was teaching the guys right out of the Bible and loving on them, but it's hard to avoid. You're like, wow, that's Kobe Bryant or Lebron or Shaq.

But in my second season it finally registered: it sank in that I was really the pastor to these guys, and these guys are real people, and just like all of us, they need love and guidance, direction, counsel, and friendship. If you cut them, they bleed. And many of them are bleeding, just like the rest of us. If I was going to make a difference in the lives of these players, it would only come through *influence*. The more I focused on influencing the players in a positive way, the more I saw amazing things happen.

Influence opens more doors than power.

Through the years, Natalie and I have had more "ministry moments" than I can count. She and I have had dinner with the players and their wives, gotten to know them, and heard about the struggles they face. Yes, professional athletes, even with their generous compensation packages, have struggles. I've had them come to me to say they're married and have kids but have gotten another woman pregnant while on the road—devastating news and heartbreaking scenarios. I've received phone calls when athletes have been arrested. Even with all of the money coming in—many of these guys make *millions* of dollars a year—they're broke. They literally have more money going out than coming in and face overwhelming financial hardship.

Sometimes their financial pressures are a direct result of a family member bleeding them dry. Other times, it's a "financial advisor" who is ripping them off instead of protecting their assets. More than one has called to ask me for a hospital visit because they are having surgery for an injury that could end their sports career—extremely scary stuff. Sometimes, the phone call isn't about them at all but about their child who needs surgery or a parent that is close to death. Through all of those desperate circumstances, I have come to realize that every phone call is an opportunity, a moment, a cherished privilege for me to be a person of *influence*. But there is only one way to become a person of influence to people who are hurting. You must be genuine, real, *authentic*, or they can see you coming a mile away.

Real Recognizes Real

People in the world of celebrities and high-flying athletes have a very small circle of trust, and who can blame them? They have been burned, over and over, by people who only see them as a wallet, not a person. They are burned out on people who smile and give them enormous compliments, only to find out it was just a put-on.

Jerry Colangelo is a stellar example of a person of influence. Most anything that has to do with professional sports in Phoenix has Jerry Colangelo's fingerprints all over it. It almost seems that it was his destiny to bring "big" sports to the desert—and to bring the World Series trophy here for the Arizona Diamondbacks. Jerry has accomplished some astounding things. At one time, he owned the Phoenix Suns, he was the former managing general partner of the Arizona Diamondbacks, and he was instrumental in bringing the Phoenix Coyotes to town as well as the Women's National Basketball Association team, the Phoenix Mercury.

Not only is Jerry Colangelo a brilliant businessman, he has an amazing heart for ministry. He has served as president of the Phoenix-area Big Brothers organization and as chairman of the board for the Christian Businessmen's Club. He faithfully attends his church and has been named Entrepreneur of the Year or Executive of the Year by numerous organizations, including the NBA.

As a college basketball player at the University of Illinois, Colangelo earned all Big Ten honors, averaging fifteen points per game during his career there. Captain of the team, he was later inducted into the Illinois Basketball Hall of Fame.

Mr. Colangelo began his business career as director of merchandising and head scout for the Chicago Bulls in 1966, and in 1968, he moved to Arizona where he assumed the general manager position with the Phoenix Suns. After his run as GM—and several years as head coach—he led a group in 1987 that purchased the franchise, for which he became president and CEO until 2005.

Colangelo's vision for a sports arena in Phoenix became a shining reality in 1992. Under his direction and management, America West Arena (now the US Airways Arena) is the centerpiece of a downtown revitalization process for Phoenix. In March 1995, he was awarded a major league baseball franchise, and the Arizona Diamondbacks took the field in 1998. The team's home field—Bank One ballpark, or BOB—has since been renamed Chase Field, a $350 million ball park with retractable roof and natural grass. And literally in record time, his brand new expansion team won the 2001 World Series by beating a proud and cocky New York Yankees team in game seven. So in Jerry Colangelo, we are talking about one of the premiere movers and shakers in Phoenix, Arizona.

Yet Jerry Colangelo's life story is not about everything going right every time. It's a story about someone making the best of every opportunity God brought his way. Because he's credited with making the Suns and the Diamondbacks a success, most of us have probably forgotten his *failed* attempts to birth a local soccer team. Anybody remember the Arizona Sandsharks? Or how about the Phoenix Smash of World Team Tennis? I doubt it.

Being a person of influence doesn't mean that everything you touch turns to gold. Influence isn't about success; it's about using what God has given you *to bless other people.*

Jerry Colangelo grew up in a part of Chicago Heights known as Hungry Hill. Does that sound like a wealthy, silver-spoon-in-your-mouth neighborhood? Hardly. But it gives one particular quote from Jerry Colangelo's book, *How You Play the Game,* special significance. It will give you some insight into why he's been successful:

> I started my way at the bottom, and have worked my way to a position where I have been able to

> fulfill many of my ambitions, and achieve many
> of my goals. I didn't use secrets, or a trust fund,
> or magic. I used whatever abilities God granted
> me, and I worked harder, and then harder still.

While some big sports team owners show little regard for their players and are known for *not* keeping promises, Colangelo's players and associates vouch that Jerry always keeps his word. For instance, Cotton Fitzsimmons, who coached the Suns for Colangelo and served as the team's vice president and announcer, once said, "You don't need a contract with Jerry if you have his word. He's as honest a man as you could ever want to be associated with." Colangelo's good reputation is so well-known, in fact, that he actually has players calling him to ask if they can play on one of his teams.

Colangelo believes the main reason he's succeeded in Arizona is his commitment to community service. He believes that, as his players and other employees become more involved in the community, the fans will reciprocate. Colangelo's autobiography, *How You Play the Game*, has been a best-seller, but he doesn't get a cent from the book sales. All of his royalties go to programs for youth, the homeless, and the elderly in the state of Arizona.

Colangelo always recommends that up-and-coming entrepreneurs get involved in community service. He supports a staggering number of community activities and organizations. He has founded, led, taught in, or otherwise supported organizations for the homeless, children, the arts, and downtown revitalization.

Consider Jerry's perspective as he explained in his acceptance speech for the 1997 Outstanding Business Leader of the Year Award:

> One of the things that I've felt was very, very important in my life was keeping a balance and keeping priorities in place. We can talk about achievements; they come, and they go. Fortunes are made and fortunes are lost, but I do believe if you maintain the right balance, you have a better chance to have a successful life. In my case, it's a matter of prioritizing what's most important to me. And that is my faith, my family, and then business.

What's the secret to having great influence? Keeping your priorities in the right order: faith, family, and *then* business. God can do great things when your priorities align with His.

Prime Time—and Not so Prime Time—Influencers

Jerry Colangelo is an influencer. But God is at work not only among "prime time" movers and shakers, but also in helping *everyone*—including you!—achieve his or her destiny. Ephesians 2:10 says, "We are God's workmanship, created in Christ Jesus to do good works, which God prepared in advance for us to do."

I have one more story about radical influence. It's about Tim Tebow. Love him or hate him, his influence overflows.

I had a chance to interview Tim at our church on Super Bowl Sunday in 2013. Many people who saw it live or watched the video online have said that it was a phenomenal interchange. As you listen to him, you are struck by the feeling you are hearing a genuinely awesome guy.

God has good things already designed for you to accomplish, and He's perfectly created you to get the job done!

At the time Tebow spoke at our church, he was the focus of a lot of national media attention because he hadn't yet been picked up by an NFL team, and some people were saying that his NFL days were over. Others speculated that he was in the Scottsdale area for a specific reason, and his visit stirred all the conjecture and guessing that goes with the rumors about signing and trading players. So, our church interview with Tebow made it into the national media. It landed on the home page of MSN.com. It was in *USA Today*. We couldn't have asked for a more amazing set up and were truly blessed with a position of major influence through that interview.

We had worked on getting Tebow booked at the church, but never in our wildest dreams did we think it would work out to occur on Super Bowl Sunday. It was the most fantastic timing imaginable! Even so, the influence of that one interview blew beyond anything I could have ever dreamed.

Bruce McClellan, a buddy of mine who played for the Kansas City Royals back in 2003, now lives in Africa where he saw the MSN.com article about the Tim Tebow interview. Intrigued by what he read, McClellan tracked me down online and sent me an email:

> Man, Pastor Travis, I don't know if you
> remember me? My name is Bruce McClellan. I
> used to play with the Kansas City Royals. I saw
> the article, and you know, I heard about you
> interviewing Tim Tebow, and I heard about
> your church. I just want you to know that I serve
> in ministry today in Africa because of your
> ministry to the Kansas City Royals ten years ago.

I was floored. My eyes filled with tears as I read Bruce's email. How could I have known that, while I was standing in the Royals locker room, strumming my guitar, not really having any idea of what I was doing, that I was influencing a pro athlete who would later go into ministry in Africa? *Ten years earlier*, I had a profound influence on a guy—even in my rookie year as a chaplain—who went on to do great and God-honoring things with his life, and now, here he was, crediting it back to me—to *my* influence!

God let me hear about a story about my influence that I didn't even know existed. Although Bruce had been in ministry for years, I had no idea, and it makes me wonder how many more stories like that might be out there. His is the kind of story that really puts a smile on your face and makes you proud to be serving on team Jesus. It also keeps you fighting and moving on. But here's the main point:

At times, you might think you have made absolutely no progress. Have you ever had one of *those* days? It seems like you're mired down in the mundane muck of life, but I want you to realize that sometimes, precisely because you are doing the mundane, you are actually setting the stage for a huge influence on somebody, and you don't even know it. Don't ever doubt the influence you have on people. Don't ever think you won't make a mark on this world.

You won't always realize that your small act of service which has faded from memory is still profoundly influencing someone—and that they're influencing someone else because of your influence.

Look at Michael J. Fox, a man battling Parkinson's Disease, and yet, in 2013, he launched a new television series that doesn't try to hide his struggle but makes it a part of the plot. All around you, people are just waiting for you to inspire them, to motivate them, to change the course of their lives for the better. You might think your influence is not that significant. You may think life is all about just "getting by." You might even believe the best thing you can do is just crawl in a hole and hide for the rest of your life. But if you think any of those things, you, my friend, are mistaken. You are a game changer in every sense of the word—more amazing than words can describe!

Don't ever, ever, ever think you are not an influencer. You can be the most amazing influencer to ever walk across this earth, and it's time for you to step into your position of influence!

You are going to rearrange your priorities to find a new level of success, significance, and influence. You are going to make some serious changes in your life—right now.

I hope you feel a gigantic expectancy, an unmanageable urgency birthing in your soul to change some things in your life for the better. There are people and things that you need to evaluate, because they are not aligned with God's favor, plans, and blessing for your future. You are going to start pouring over God's Word, searching out His truths, and applying His ways to your life, priorities, relationships, and work. You are never going to be the same after reading this chapter on influence. Okay? Although you may have once seen yourself as merely a pawn in the chess game, now you know you are the chess *player*, and it's time to make your move!

I hope you'll look back at this time in your life and remember that you heard a life-changing message from God as you read this chapter and that you have no time to waste. You are now on a mission! The story has not yet been written about the amazing ways in which you will influence other people who will, in turn, influence others all over the world—just because of your influence on them!

Prayer for Influence

Dear Jesus,

I don't want to be merely a success in life. I want to have significance. Right now, You are gently speaking to my heart, showing me areas of my life You want to adjust and change, so my priorities will be in line with Your plan for my future. I willingly submit myself to Your changes in my heart and soul, and I ask You to make me a great influencer for You. Take my small start, and help me see every day as a gift, every meeting as an opportunity, and every person as an awesome collaborator I can influence profoundly. Please keep my spiritual eyes open for unexpected ways in which You will do this.

In Jesus Name. Amen.

Scriptures to Reflect on

1 Timothy 4:12
Proverbs 25:15
2 Chronicles 34:32-33

Chapter 12

FAITH

"It's easy to have faith in yourself and have discipline when you're a winner, when you're number one. What you've got to have is faith and discipline when you're not a winner."

—VINCE LOMBARDI, COACH OF THE GREEN BAY PACKERS AND WINNER OF THREE CONSECUTIVE NFL CHAMPIONSHIPS

Featured Disciple:
Thomas, the "doubting disciple," who had to learn to have faith.

"Now faith is the substance of things hoped for, the evidence of things not seen."
Hebrews 11:1

Faith is "confident belief in the truth, value, or trustworthiness of a person, idea, or thing; belief that does not rest on logical proof or material evidence; the theological virtue defined as secure belief in God and a trusting acceptance of God's will."
[www.thefreedictionary.com]

In George Michael's 1988 hit song, "Faith", he gets a lot of things messed up. But there is one thing he does get right. He tells us over and over again that he's got to have faith.

You can't make it through life without having faith. But the question is: faith in what? Let's talk about that.

Lighten Up

Formal surveys and informal conversations both confirm that the single most common reason people give for moving to Arizona boils down to one word: *sunshine*. People love the sunshine, the light, and the uplifting feeling it gives them.

Light is a major theme in the Bible, and 1 John 1:5 tells why: "God is light and in Him is no darkness at all."

The very first command God gave in creation was, "Let there be light." And later, Jesus told His disciples, "I am the light of the world." Jesus is all about light coming to a dark, cloudy world.

The fact is, life disappoints us sometimes. Things don't always work out as planned. Situations don't always come together for a happy ending. Like me, you could probably tell your share of those stories.

I imagine the disciples were extremely discouraged during the final days and hours of Jesus' life. They had hoped Jesus would be the political leader to overthrow the Roman government. Here was someone who could heal people, feed thousands, give blind people their sight, and who could explain the Old Testament scriptures with complete authority. However, just days after Jesus rode through the streets of Jerusalem in a triumphant parade, He was *crucified*—an embarrassing, degrading, tortuous death reserved for the most wicked of criminals. Can you imagine the disciples' free fall, from optimism to devastation?

One of the great follow-on stories of Easter is that of "doubting Thomas," a disciple who didn't believe Jesus had actually risen from the dead. He was a realist and told the others, "Hey, unless I see His scarred hands and actually stick my hand into the wound in the side of His body, I can't believe it!"

Not long after laying out his conditions for belief, Thomas was with the disciples again when Jesus suddenly appeared. He made a beeline for Thomas and told him, "Since you're the one telling everybody you have some serious doubts, go ahead and check out the wounds in My hands and side. This really is Me, and I have really come back to life!" In that moment, Thomas went from major doubts, to *major* faith, and all he could think to say was, "My Lord and My God!" The awe-inspiring light of Jesus overwhelmed him.

I think Thomas gets a bad rap and a bad name for something we've all done: doubt Jesus. Each of us has been a doubting Thomas or doubting Travis at one point or another, but having faith moves us from the darkness of doubt into the light. Here's the crazy thing about darkness and light: we have a choice about which one to live in.

You can remain in the cloudy, dark nights of life, or you can choose to step out and live in the light. God shines the sunlight on everybody—the Bible tells us that—but you can withdraw into your own little hideaway, disconnected from people and away from the sun. It's up to you. God won't force the light on you. You can put on the blindfold and say, "I'm not going to move forward; I'm not going to live in the light." And you can welcome darkness to take over your whole existence.

Faithing the Giants

In the final days of 1991, the world watched, astounded, as the communist superpower known as the Soviet Union split apart at the seams. As the nation unraveled, *Time* magazine ran this quote from Mikhail Gorbachev, the last president of the Soviet Union:

> We, in the Soviet Union, have changed our opinion on some matters such as religion. The moral values that Christianity has generated and embodied for centuries can help in the work of renewal for our country.

Wow. Did you get that? It's not Billy Graham or Greg Laurie or Rick Warren saying that. It's a one-time *communist* politician and government official! "Hey," he's saying, "We figured it out: Christianity is legit after all."

For years, the communist regime in the Soviet Union tried to eradicate even the most miniscule ripple of spirituality in Russia. Yet the light of Jesus finally erased their doubts and flung open the doors to the amazing grace of God's love.

When you face a roadblock or a situation that looks like it is never going to get better, look out! That is when God loves to do a miracle *bigger* than anything you could possibly imagine. And it always starts with faith, with the light of Jesus Christ.

I don't know what giants you're facing, but keep the faith. Like Hebrews 11:1 says, "Now faith is the substance of things hoped for, the evidence of things not seen." What a great Bible verse—simple but loaded with depth.

Of course, you can't see faith. Before faith does its job, things don't look like what they're going to look like. You can't see faith—or what it produces—physically, but you can see it mentally. You believe for it and pray for it.

Impact Church is built on faith. We've seen tons of miracles happen when we couldn't imagine how they could possibly happen. Some of the giants in our path seemed like show-stoppers, and if we had looked at them for too long, our "show" would have ground to a halt. The lesson is:

If you're looking at the giants in your life, this will set you free: *Stop lookin' at 'em!*

Instead, envision what God is going to do. Hope, believe, pray. And have faith! Second Corinthians 5:7 points out how it works: "For we walk by faith, and not by sight." Martin Luther King Jr. had a great way of looking at this: "Faith is taking the first step when you can't see the whole staircase."

What is your giant today? Whatever it is, stop staring at the giants, and start seeing the giant *miracles* for your life. It's all about focusing on faith. Take your eyes off the wrong thing, and set them on the right thing, the God thing. He specializes in the impossible.

I've seen him do it time and time again. Right after we married, Natalie and I helped a church get started, and God did some crazily miraculous stuff there. We grew from zero—nada, nobody—to *six thousand* people in attendance every weekend in just eight years! The place just absolutely blew up.

During our twelve years as part of that miracle church, I also started serving the Phoenix Suns as their team pastor. In 2002, the same year I took on my role with the Suns, I began spring training chapels with the Kansas City Royals. After eight years with the Royals, I was "traded" to the Oakland A's for a better contract. It wasn't much of a trade, of course, since team chaplains don't get paid, and there's no draft. But I did switch teams to serve closer to home.

About the same time, we made another bold move. I became pastor of Desert Life Church on July 25, 2010, and it was a scary change. We left the security of twelve-and-a-half years of a church and people that we loved. My daughter Kylie was nine when we left, and my son Josiah was seven. They were born into the church and didn't know any other. At the time we arrived on the scene at Desert Life, the whole church was made up of a couple hundred people. Our kids were used to having sixteen hundred children in the kids ministry *alone*, and at Desert Life, there were only two dozen children.

And there were "giants in the land." The church was in a mess, mostly because the economy was a mess. When people lose their jobs, they don't get paid. And guess what happens when they don't get paid? They don't tithe; they don't give offerings to the Lord because they can't. And when that happens, the church suffers financially, too. And Desert Life was suffering—big time! It was in foreclosure!

Foreclosure notices arrived in the mail once a week, and we were getting phone calls from the bank every single day. "We're going to shut the doors on you," they chided. "You have to make the payment." We were behind by three mortgage payments, plus fees—more than $90,000! There was no way we could pay it. It was our biggest giant.

The financial mess also reflected the physical state of the church building. It was a near disaster. I've seen frat houses with carpet in better condition than the church. It was full of stains and holes and probably a bunch of other stuff I don't want to know about after years of neglect. It was *bad*.

The building needed to be remodeled, but we had zero dollars to do it. We told God, "Lord, we want to do it, we can see it, we have a vision for it, but we can't do it. There just isn't the money to do it. But we know, God, that *You* can do it."

The roof was bad, too, and needed to be replaced. The air conditioning units needed to be replaced—none of them cooled well, and some didn't work at all. The exterior paint—what there was of it—was bad. The parking lot was bad. Are you picking up on the theme here? *Bad*. Really bad.

The church leadership and I decided to launch a campaign with a sermon series called "We Believe" to try and raise a little money. This in spite of the fact pastor friends have warned that if you're a new pastor, you shouldn't do any fund-raising in the first twelve months because people don't trust you yet, and you just need to relax and win people over—to love on them. But I told our church, "We have to! We've got to raise some money— at least $100,000!" So we set a goal of a hundred grand to just do some basic remodeling. It wouldn't get us very far, but it would help.

During the campaign, we fell short of our goal and raised only $60,000—and that was even with one person donating $20,000 of the total. But God had an interesting idea. Right about that same time, a major hailstorm blew through North Scottsdale. Nothing in Scottsdale seemed to escape without severe damage. Cars everywhere drove around with golf-ball size dents all over them, and when the storm hit it blasted our already bad building. (Have I mentioned that the building was in bad shape?) Hail scratched off most of the remaining paint, it pounded our roof into scrap, and any working air conditioning unit was destroyed. But guess what: as bad a shape as our building had been in, the church still had property insurance. We filed an insurance claim, and our "We Believe" campaign turned into the "Hail, Yeah!" campaign. Heaven used hail as our game changer.

Desert Life received an insurance check for over $250,000! That, coupled with the $60,000 we had already raised, allowed us to remodel the entire building—the carpet, chairs, lobby, ceiling tiles, the stage, the exterior, the A/C units, even the asphalt in the parking lot. How cool is that? We not only repaired the storm damage but we also fixed and remodeled everything that needed to be done!

We had also started to grow a little in attendance, but the big giant still hovered over us: foreclosure. When the insurance and campaign money flowed in, some people asked me, "Don't you think we should catch up on the mortgage payments?" But I told them, "I don't think so."

While I could see the potential wisdom in that, I knew we needed to get the building up to date if we wanted anyone to attend. After all, we were in Scottsdale, Arizona. But the foreclosure thing was down to the wire. The bank had said, "You have thirty days to catch up, or else that's a wrap!"

My executive associate pastor, Andre Wadsworth, and I were frustrated, discouraged, fearful, and yet we were also full of faith and hope. We told God, "Lord, you didn't bring us this far to watch us drop off a cliff—or maybe you did. We don't know, but we'll do whatever You want us to do!"

I also did my best to keep a light-hearted attitude. The Scottsdale airport sat next to the church, so I kept telling Andre and our church, "Well, if we do fly this sucker into the ground, at least we are on the runway."

Finally, I came up with an idea I shared with Andre. "Pastor Andre," I said, "we need to fly to California, get in front of our bankers, fall on our faces, cry for mercy, and show them some charts and graphs of our recent growth, and outline our vision for the church. Let's just see what they say."

His response amazed me: "You know what? I've been thinking the same thing."

Yet even to try my save-the-church plan, we needed money, and the church was broke. Pastor Andre and I weren't even getting paid. In fact, he and I were putting our own money into the church out of our savings accounts. But that wasn't end-of-story. A church member donated "buddy passes," so we could make the flight to California to see the bankers. Thank God for people in church who work for airlines!

At our presentation, the bankers just stared at us with their arms folded, like bankers do. Andre and I didn't know what to make of it. We didn't say much on the way back to the airport, and when we got there, I said, "Man, that didn't go as well as we had hoped." You might say that was an understatement. So we flew back to Phoenix, feeling pretty glum.

The next day, though, in what we thought was our darkest hour, we had a game-changing moment. The bank called, and the loan manager for the church mortgage said to me, "Pastor Travis, I want you to know that we really appreciate you guys flying over to see us. People just don't do that. We very impressed, and we really appreciate the vision, the charts, and your transparency—and *we want to work with you.*"

I about fell out! My eyes filled with tears. I was so overwhelmed with God's favor and protection, I cried like a three-year-old girl, lip quivering, chin quivering, and everything.

The banker didn't seem to notice as he continued, "This is what we want to do: Your payment is about $23,000 per month right now. We want to restructure your payment, and it will drop to $14,800 per month. We're dropping the interest rate. We're going to modify the whole thing. Also, Pastor Travis, you're behind almost $100,000 in payments and fees. So, we're going to wipe that clean—we're just going to make it go away. Then, on top of that, you have a second-mortgage line-of-credit of $350,000 on your property with us—a fairly sizeable second mortgage. That second that you have—that 'B-note'? We're just going to zero that out as well."

Still listening to the banker while crying and grinning ear to ear, I walked into Andre's office. He took one look at me and asked, "Are you all right, Pastor Trav?"

I whispered back, "Yeah, I'm awesome, and this is crazy. This is a game-changer, bro. Wait till you hear this. I can hardly wait to tell you." The banker even gave us several months without any payments as the restructure of our loan took place, so we could get ahead.

Since then, we changed the name Desert Life to Impact Church and "rebranded" the church. We've also watched God do the impossible, over and over again.

How many people do you know whose bank has said it would literally forgive you your debts and start over—like Jesus would do? As far as I know, that just doesn't happen.

Other giants also confronted the church during my first year there. Our amazingly gifted and skilled worship leader stepped down and moved to California. This remarkable woman had done three jobs in one for us. She was worship leader, receptionist, and the youth pastor's wife. When she left, I wondered, "God, what are we going to do now?"

What we did was to begin an international search for a music pastor. Who we found was Michael Land. He was a musician in Alaska, working as a plumber. When I first heard his music, I called and said, "Really, dude, I'm pretty sure God has not designed you to be a plumber. You're working with the *wrong pipes*, bro! You need to be singing for Jesus!"

And I hired what I am convinced is the most talented and competent worship pastor in America. If you haven't heard him or checked him out, go to impactchurch.com and click on the ImpactTV link. You will be blessed!

I don't know what your giant is today,
but I encourage you to keep believing,
to keep the faith!

While God brews the miracles, we use our brains and do all we can to work things out, but at the end of the day, it's God's deal. That's why I believe in faith.

Even the amazing story of how God rescued Impact Church from foreclosure and bankruptcy still does not compare with the story of how people come to know Jesus Christ as Lord and Savior. Our church growth trend continued, and during the twelve months following our near-foreclosure, we grew by 904 people—155 percent! We more than doubled in size! It's unheard of, but here's why that's happening: because people are being "impacted" by the Holy Spirit and the power of Jesus Christ. When was the last time you went to church and watched 149 people get baptized in water? God is doing something cool at Impact Church!

Imperfect Faith in a Perfect God

I am on Instagram (@travishearn), and I love to check out the hashtags to see what people are saying about #ImpactChurch. Many of them post pictures of their filled-in bulletin outlines, comments about the worship team, and especially our baptism of 149 people. One post in particular caught my eye, the caption to a picture of somebody being baptized:

> So I went to church this morning to witness baptism day, but I never imagined that I would recommit my life to Jesus and get in the tank myself.

Or this one:

> Today is a day I'll never forget. Today is the day
> I gave my life to Christ, and today I was baptized
> at Impact Church.

That never gets old! I could hear hundreds of stories like that. You show up at church, grab a doughnut, sip some coffee, listen to the band and think, "Wow, they're pretty good." The next thing you know, God runs you over like a freight train, and you're in the water getting baptized in front of a bunch of people you don't even know!

Although none of us at church, on our staff, or in our homes are perfect, we serve a God who is. We have faith, not in who *we* are, but in who *God* is. I will let you down, whether I'm your pastor, friend, or relative. Our church staff will let you down because all of us are fallible.

You're not perfect, either, and right now, I know the game-changing solution for any disaster you might be facing or for whatever impossible situation you can't solve. The solution is . . . *have faith!* Faith is the game changer. The way you build up your faith is by hearing God's Word, to read about all the people in the Bible who also went through crazy times. When they had faith, the impossible came true.

Read about Abraham and Sarah, for instance, who were too old to have children, yet God provided a miracle baby in their old age. Check out Gideon, who was a total wimp, and yet God used him as a mighty warrior. Then there's the crazy story about Joshua having to follow in the footsteps of the icon, Moses, and yet he brought down the walls of an enemy city by marching around it seven times to the tune of a praise-and-worship concert. You can read about David, who defeated the giant Goliath with a slingshot. There's the totally cool story of Hezekiah, who laid his requests out before God and didn't have to lift a finger to defeat his enemies. The list is too long to keep going, but these should motivate you to grab a Bible and start filling yourself full of stories of amazing faith. The reason some people *lose* faith is that they aren't reading enough Bible stories *about* faith.

But I have every confidence you aren't going to be one of those people. Why? You are a game changer! You are going to walk by *faith* not by sight, and you are going to change the world with your incredible faith.

I hope you are ready to make a commitment to walk the rest of your life by faith. That means, when you see seemingly insurmountable problems building up in your life, you will remind yourself that what you see is *not* what you get. You will say to yourself, "I am only going to glance at those circumstances, those details, those problems, and I am now going to put one foot in front of another and walk by *faith!*"

Prayer for Faith

Dear Jesus,

Every day is a choice. The moment my feet hit the floor, I have a decision to make: walk by what I can see or walk by faith. Today, I commit to taking a stand, to walking by faith. I am going to stop looking at the giants in my life and start seeing the giant miracles You're going to do. I am going to fill myself up with faith in You and walk in confidence and power. I am never going to be the same again. I will walk in humility but full of power that comes from having faith that You will do amazing things through me and in me. Even when I see an insurmountable wall in front of me and it looks like there is no way around it, I am going to trust in You, knowing that You have my best interests at heart and that if the wall doesn't fall down, it's time to start looking for the tunnel or the hang-glider You will provide to take me under it or over it. In the name of Jesus, I pray for great faith to invade my heart, and let it be a powerful presence all around me. Let people notice the crazy change You are doing in me today.

In Jesus Name. Amen.

Scriptures to Reflect on

Psalm 6
1 Timothy 6:12
Hebrews 11:1

Chapter 13

TIMING

"I skate where the puck is going to be,
not where it has been."

—WAYNE GRETZKY, "THE GREAT,"
ALL-STAR HOCKEY PLAYER

Featured Disciple:
Matthias, the thirteenth disciple who was picked to replace
Judas Iscariot after Jesus ascended into heaven.

"But you must not forget this one thing, dear friends:
A day is like a thousand years to the Lord, and a
thousand years is like a day. The Lord isn't really
being slow about his promise, as some people think.
No, he is being patient for your sake."
2 Peter 3:8-9a (NLT)

Timing is "the regulation of occurrence, pace,
or coordination to achieve a desired effect, as in music,
the theater, athletics, or mechanics."
[www.thefreedictionary.com]

I'm sure you've heard people say, "Timing is everything," but man, sometimes I hate to wait for that timing, don't you? I always want to just get after it, make it happen, and get the job done. But the most amazing moments happen when it all comes together in *God's timing*.

God doesn't ever seem to be in a hurry. *We* may be, but *God* is not. We might think we have just one opportunity, but God can *make* a new opportunity any time He wants to. We might think we've missed the window, but God can create a new window. In God's timing, something good can be replaced by something *greater*.

Thirteenth Time's a Charm

Think about that dude, Matthias, disciple number thirteen. You might say, "Wait a minute. I thought there were just twelve disciples." And you would be right. But after Judas betrayed Jesus, the Bible says he was filled with deep remorse, so he went out and hung himself. So in a way, there was an "opening" on the roster for a replacement disciple.

After Jesus ascended into heaven, the disciples had to pick a replacement, so that they could roll with twelve again. Their only requirement was that the new guy had to have been around for the whole time Jesus was ministering. They wanted somebody who had witnessed everything that had happened—the miracles, the healings, the crucifixion, the resurrection—all of it. Apparently, Matthias fit the job description. He was around during the entire ministries of both John the Baptist and Jesus. He saw all of it, but at the beginning, he was not picked to be "one of the twelve." He was down a level in the organization.

In fact, Judas Iscariot, the traitor, beat him out to be one of the original twelve.

He was a second-string disciple. Matthias came off the bench after the Hall-of-Fame coach, Jesus, retired. He didn't get on the field during regulation play. He got into the game in overtime, after Jesus had ascended into heaven. Acts 1:24-26 tells us the way in which he was chosen as a thirteenth round draft pick:

> Then they prayed, "Lord, you know everyone's
> heart. Show us which of these two you have
> chosen to take over this apostolic ministry,
> which Judas left to go where he belongs." Then
> they cast lots, and the lot fell to Matthias; so he
> was added to the eleven apostles. (Acts 1:24-26)

Can you imagine the feelings he might have had? "Oh man, that's cold. That's jacked up. Why couldn't Jesus have chosen me while He was still around? I missed all the good stuff!" But the truth is, *it's all good*!

Even though Matthias wasn't called one of *the* disciples from the beginning, hey, he got to be a disciple. *In God's timing*, he made the team. And his name made it into the Bible! How do we know it was God's timing? There's a tiny section in the verses right before the selection process that tells the other part of Matthias' cool story:

> "For," said Peter, "it is written in the Book of
> Psalms: 'May his place be deserted; let there be
> no one to dwell in it,' and, 'May another take his
> place of leadership.'" (Acts 1:20)

The first part of the verse refers to the field in which Judas was buried. It became a place of desolation that nobody visited. But the second part of the verse, "may another take his place of leadership," is written about the thirteenth disciple, Matthias. Thousands of years earlier, God picked Matthias to be number thirteen, and King David wrote about it in Psalm 109: 8. Isn't that incredible? God's timing took nine hundred years to be just right for Matthias to become a disciple. (Thank God most of the things we pray for won't take *that* long, right?) We have to rest in the fact that God's timing is perfect.

Having the Time of Your Life

In the last few years, God's timing has been incredible to watch. What always astounds me is how God lets us move ahead with our plans and then comes along and changes it all for the better. He almost seems to be saying, "I know you *thought* that was the right way, but let Me show you now what is *actually* the right way to get this done."

If there's one area where God has proven this to me, it's in the area of our building and expansion plans for Impact Church. The day I first pulled into the Desert Life parking lot, I already had my eyes on a nearby property. It was an abandoned car dealership right smack in the middle of the Scottsdale Airpark and right next door to the number one busiest Costco in the state of Arizona.

I told Natalie and Pastor Andre, "That would make the perfect church property." To which Andre responded, "It's crazy you're saying that, because I've thought the same thing for a long time."

Timing has always been everything and now is our game changer. While we were in foreclosure on our first property, behind on our monthly payments, and basically broke, we had no business looking into buying a twelve-acre piece of property in the middle of the Scottsdale Airpark with plenty of parking and land. It would have been outrageous to say, "Let's buy that property over *there* for $10 million" when we couldn't even handle the $3 million building we already had. Not only that, the property was never actually for sale. Nothing about the timing was right.

The property was in escrow with a developer who wanted to put a high-end luxury apartment complex with more than seven hundred units on the property. However, the city zoning process never approved the proposal, so the sale fell out of escrow.

Immediately after the apartment builders pulled out, another company, Fry's Electronics, took an escrow on it. Several months later, that deal fell through. Then Mack Truck barrels into the picture and plops a quarter-of-a-million dollars into escrow, saying, "We want to put a Mack Truck dealership on this property."

Meanwhile, we were in escrow, settling for an empty furniture store building across town in Phoenix at Tatum and Thunderbird. We had the people who could do a great remodel, the property had dynamite visibility, and even though it was in pretty bad shape, we said, "We can do this!"

So we began the due diligence process, and our ninety days for that coincided with the Mack Truck escrow timing on the other property. Realtors, attorneys, brokers, and property inspectors surrounded us with their wisdom about the abandoned furniture store, and finally, through the collective advice of all of them together, we didn't feel comfortable about closing on the deal.

God leads you in the right timing by giving you supernatural peace about moving forward. If you don't have peace, then you should be sure not to move ahead.

A few days before our planned closing date, I had a dream. I hadn't been thinking about the property Mack Truck was buying, but I dreamed that Mack Truck pulled out of their deal. Now bear in mind that I don't put a lot of stock in dreams. I usually find myself asking, "Was that God? Was that the devil? Was it the pizza I ate last night?" Although I'm not a big "dream person," this time I just couldn't shake it.

I called a good buddy of mine—a key player on what I call my "wisdom team." He's been involved in real estate for his whole career, he's an amazing thinker, he loves God, he loves me, and he loves Impact Church. In a word, he's *solid*. I trust him with my life. He had also been helping us with every detail on the furniture property, so right after I woke up from the dream—about seven in the morning—I called him and said, "Tony, I had this crazy dream that Mack Truck pulled out of the deal on the car dealership property."

"You did?"

"Yeah, they probably didn't, but just entertain me: can you look into it?"

"Yeah sure, I'll look into it," he concluded our conversation.

Tony sent an email to Volkswagen Credit, the ones holding the note on the property, and asked, "What's the deal? Is Mack Truck still closing?"

The first sentence of the return email said, "Hi Tony. Funny you should ask today, because just yesterday, Mack Truck sent over a cancellation notice. They're out."

Ummm: game changer!

Our real estate situation suddenly got as chaotic as Donkey Kong throwing back ding dongs. The asking price was $9 million, but with our notorious negotiating skills, we got them to drop all the way down to . . . $8.5 million. We went into escrow needing way more money than we had. I had no idea how we were going to come up with that amount. And that was just to acquire the property! After that, we would need millions more to build it out! But as you and I both know: when God is in it, there is no limit.

We forged ahead, not knowing how we would make the deal happen. We negotiated for eleven months of escrow because the property zoning wouldn't allow the construction of a church, and we knew the re-zoning alone could take six to nine months. So the seller gave us more time to close the deal. In the process, Volkswagen Credit made us an offer: "If you put down half the sales price in cash, we'll finance the other half—$4.25 million—at 3.25 percent interest, amortized over twenty-five years." Were they kidding? Why in the world would Volkswagen Credit be willing to finance a church? But: game changer again! That meant we needed only $4.25 million for the down payment.

Still, I found myself asking, "How in the world do we do this? It's unheard of for a church to raise a monumental amount of money like that in just ten months." I sure didn't want to step onto the stage every Sunday telling everybody, "Hey, you know the commitment and offering you gave last Sunday? Well, it's not enough. You'll have to dig deeper." I told God, "I'll do whatever you ask of me, except, Lord, I just don't think that's my cup of tea."

But God wasn't through pitching game-changers at me just yet. Remember the apartment complex? Well, they remembered the property, too, and approached us with an idea: "Years ago," they reminded us, "we tried to buy the property you're in escrow on but got shut down because zoning restrictions wouldn't allow us to put apartments on the property since it's in the 'flight zone' of the Scottsdale Airpark. But actually only *part* of the property is in the flight zone. If you draw a line from left to right across the center of the property, the back half is *not* in the flight zone. So how about if we purchase the back half from you for $1 million an acre, and you can have the frontage on Hayden? We'll do a simultaneous closing, and when we pay you $5.6 million for the back half, $4.25 million of that can go to Volkswagen Credit for your down payment, and you get the rest in cash."

Somebody was really giving some thought to this concept, but I said, "I don't know. I'll have to call our architect to see, because we have already laid out plans for the whole property— *big* plans. You're cutting the property in half. I'll have to see about it. Be patient with me."

Maybe I needed *them* to be patient, but I sure wasn't about to be! I called the church architect and told him, "I need to know, *tonight*, if we can fit the church we need to build on just the front half of the property. So, if you can draw the whole thing out, that would be awesome."

I told him we needed at least sixty thousand square feet, enough for twelve hundred chairs, a huge lobby, a coffee shop, a bookstore, a smoothie bar, a gymnasium, and also no less than four hundred parking spaces. "Can you do it?" I asked.

He listened without comment, then finally said, "I don't know. It will take some time to find out." But he came back with the whole thing drawn up. "I did it!" he told me. "I got the whole thing drawn with everything you're wanting." Woo-hoo!

That was the good news. Then we all started thinking about how this could turn out bad. What if the city didn't want to us to do it? What if they just didn't want a church and an apartment complex to share this piece of property?

When we shared our concerns with the developers of the apartment complex, they agreed to fly in and meet together with us and the City of Scottsdale. The apartment guys brought their architect from California and their principal developer from Houston, and all of us—our "people" and our attorneys—met with city officials and the mayor, and guess what? Everybody was 100 percent on board, across the board! The only question they kept asking was, "How *fast* can you do this?

They were tired of looking at the eye sore in the airpark! Although our original church plan included remodeling the old car dealership building into something we could use, the apartment complex wanted to flatten the existing building and start over. That seemed like a waste to us at first, until we "did the math" and realized it would allow for fifteen hundred people to live on "our church property" in those apartments! Is there any better way to reach people than to have them living on the church campus?

We watched in awe as God's timing unfolded into a beautiful plan and closed on the property in Spring 2014. Not only that, through the remarkable purchase by the apartment builders and a mind-blowing appraisal in our favor on the remaining property, we began day one of ownership with just over *$4 million of equity* in the church property! Isaiah's words about waiting rang true:

> "But those who wait on the Lord shall renew
> their strength; They shall mount up with wings
> like eagles, They shall run and not be weary, They
> shall walk and not faint." (Isaiah 40:31, NKJV)

When you *wait* for God's timing, amazing things happen!

Waiting, God's Way

I don't know about you, but most of the time when I pray, I am asking God for things. But I should be basking, not asking—basking in God's presence, not asking Him for presents. Yet most of the time, I have an agenda. While I don't think that's all bad—God tells us to bring our needs to Him—there are times when I think God wishes we would come to Him *without* an agenda, that we would pray to wait for His agenda.

Waiting on the Lord is about waiting *without* a plan, an agenda, a formula, a system, or a model. Waiting on the Lord is laying all of that down and saying, "God, I have a plan, but I want You to know that You can obliterate that plan and send me wherever You want and ask me to do whatever You want. I am going to wait on Your *timing*."

You know why that kind of prayer is so important? It's because we have no idea what the future holds, but we do know who holds the future: God!

Right now, as you hold this book in your hands, I hope you will be more excited than ever about what God is going to do in your life! Matthias, disciple thirteen, had no idea his life was going to be changed in such a radical way. There was no way he could know. And it certainly didn't happen in the timing he may have wanted. When it was God's time, though, Matthias received the honor of getting to be one of the disciples, among those closest to Jesus. At the time Jesus may have been in heaven, but that doesn't mean Matthias didn't receive a special connection with Jesus through the Holy Spirit. God knew the perfect timing for Matthias, and He knows the perfect timing for you too!

I don't know what difficulties or celebrations or issues or opportunities or plans or problems are part of your life or your future right now. But I know one thing: if you will *wait upon the Lord*, he will put together a supernatural timing for your efforts that will amaze you.

From now on, you are going to be sensitive and aware and tuned in to God's timing in everything you do. You are not going to be anxious, because you know God isn't anxious. You are going to become an expert at waiting on God's long-range planning process. You are going to live each day, *one day at a time*, because you realize God could change everything for the better with one phone call, one email, one conversation, one luncheon, or one post on a blog. You are now living in confidence, walking in faith, and speaking in love, because you know God has a timing that is crazily, outrageously superior to anything you could know about or dream up. You are getting excited, even as you read this, because you sense the incredible potential God's timing has to offer.

You can't see the future, but *God can*. You can't possibly know the right answer, but God always does. You can't see a way out, but God can see a boat-load of ways out. You can't see the solution, but God has about a dozen solutions up His sleeve. You think your limitations are your downfall, but God sees your limitations as a way for His power to be perfectly displayed to the entire world. You see your lack of money as a constant drain on your feelings of security, but God sees your lack of money as a way to keep you close to Him. You see friends that seem fickle and undependable, but God sees you as a friend He will never abandon or let down.

You are going to wait for God's impeccable timing with perfect joy and excitement. You are going to whisper the name Matthias to yourself and smile because it will remind you of how your time in the sun could be right around the corner, just when you were thinking the sun had already set. *Your life is all about timing—God's timing!* Knowing that is a game changer!

Prayer for Timing

Dear Jesus,

So many things in my life seem like they have stalled out. Some days, it seems like I make no progress, but help me to see those days as opportunities to wait upon You, Lord. Teach me to wait, not with an agenda, but with expectation and an open heart. Show me how to be more sensitive to the cool ways in which You are moving and placing things into motion I could never orchestrate. Keep my heart in the right place, so I never get angry or frustrated over a delay in my plans. In fact, when a delay comes, help me turn to you and ask, "Lord, what are You doing now? What is this delay about? How do You want to use this in my life?" From this day forward, I am going to submit to Your timing for my life. I want to make sure I never get ahead of You or behind You. I want to be *in step* with You.

In Jesus Name. Amen.

Scriptures to Reflect on

Daniel 2:20-22
Jeremiah 29:11
Isaiah 30:21

Chapter 14

PURPOSE

"God places the heaviest burden on those who can carry its weight."

—REGGIE WHITE, NFL PRO FOOTBALL
HALL-OF-FAMER

Featured Disciple:
You, the disciple Jesus picked to serve God's purposes *right now*.

"Now when David had served God's purpose in his own generation, he fell asleep; he was buried with his ancestors and his body decayed."
Acts 13:36

Purpose is "the object toward which one strives or for which something exists; a result or effect that is intended or desired, an intention; the matter at hand; the point at issue."
[www.thefreedictionary.com]

I want to leave you with one last thought, and it has to do with the purpose for your life. If anybody has been a leader in bringing *purpose* into focus, it would be Pastor Rick Warren, author of *The Purpose Driven Life*. It is such a *New York Times* best-seller that it is, in fact, the best-selling non-fiction book of all time, besides the Bible itself! The book is so profound that it's hard to pick out just one quote to leave you with, so I recommend that you buy the book if you haven't done so already and read it. Rick's message is life-changing! But here is one of my all-time favorite quotes from *The Purpose Drive Life*:

> If you have felt hopeless, hold on! Wonderful
> changes are going to happen in your life as you
> begin to live it on *purpose*.

God has an amazing purpose for your life, and your most exciting times are still ahead of you. You have never yet failed to the point that God can't use you. In fact, failure is something God loves to use. Again, Rick says it best:

> If you want God to bless you and use you greatly,
> you must be willing to walk with a limp the rest
> of your life, because God uses weak people.

That is really good news for somebody like me—and probably for you, too. I walk with a few limps. You may have noticed that I've been pretty straight with you about the failures and disasters in my life. If you and I were to get together so you could tell me the things you don't like about me, I could match you, shortcoming for shortcoming, and then some! I am absolutely not someone who can throw stones, in part because I spent a good part of my early life, stoned.

But God loves to use the messed up parts of our lives to make something incredible happen. You know why? Because then *He* gets the credit. Everybody looks at you, and says things like, "There's no way Trav pulled *that* off by himself!" And they're exactly right. There is no way, but God is in the business of making a way.

Directions, on Purpose

Living your life with an understanding of the purpose God has for you is truly a game changer. There is nothing God has planned for you that He won't also provide the way, the resources, the friends, the assets, the timing, the learning, the courage, the determination, and the perseverance by which you can accomplish it. And here's the best part: that takes all the pressure off of you to make it happen. Sure, you work hard and bust your butt to make things happen, but at the end of the day, you can lay your head down on the pillow, and say, "Lord, I didn't get everything done that I wanted to today, but I am excited that I spent the day with You and that I know You a little bit better, love you a little more, and that's good enough for me!" For many people, that alone is life-changing. It means you can resign as the manager of the universe.

Isn't it amazing what has happened in the last few years with technology? I love the navigation system on my smart-phone. I can search out an address for the place I want to visit, cut and paste that address into a navigation app, and boom! I get a detailed digital display of the roadmap to my destination, accompanied with turn-by-turn directions on the phone's speaker. One of my favorite features is that, even when you miss a turn, it's still no big deal, because the little voice in the phone utters that famous word, "Recalculating!" Within seconds, you are directed from your messed up route to the goal you had in the first place. In a sense, you're never lost with a GPS system.

Perhaps you can guess what analogy is coming next, but I'll tell you that God operates the same way. Maybe right now, you can look back over your life and see a whole string of bad choices and big mistakes. You cringe over many things you're not proud of. You can barely stand to think about some of the sins and failures you've made. Some of them were secrets that became not-so-secret, and that made things even more unbearable. But here is the *good news* Jesus brings to your life and situation: "Recalculating!"

You have never strayed so far from God's grace that He can't bring things back for you. All the wrong turns in your life might be horrific, devastating, and even hard to think about, but God can take you, right where you are, and re-route you. You may actually end up closer to your goal now than you would have on your original course!

God's never in a hurry. He loves to take you through some "recalculating" scenarios, just so you don't start thinking that you've got a grip on this thing called life. The minute you start relying on yourself is when you are in more trouble than you realize.

Natalie and I have come to that place more times in our lives than I can count. We have been completely devastated with news—news that we can't get pregnant, that we may never find a baby to adopt, that our church is in foreclosure, that there isn't enough money for critical remodeling, that surgeries are needed, cars are wrecked, friends have died—all the stuff that comes at you in life. But we take seriously what the apostle Peter says about all of this:

> Dear friends, do not be surprised at the fiery
> ordeal that has come on you to test you, as though
> something strange were happening to you. But
> rejoice inasmuch as you participate in the
> sufferings of Christ, so that you may be overjoyed
> when his glory is revealed. (1 Peter 4:12-13)

For some reason, I'm still surprised when I have to go through tough stuff, but Peter says, "*don't* be surprised." His good advice will help us cope with those feelings of panic that sweep over all of us.

Get On-Purpose

You are about to enter the most amazing time of your life because you can now relax in God's care, and let Him do all the behind-the-scenes work to bring your dreams and goals into reality. Do I remember that all the time? Not a chance. I need a daily reminder that everything is under God's control. But I repeat to myself all the time: Jesus loves me; Jesus cares for me; Jesus is in control. It makes me smile every time I say that to myself.

I hope you will never be the same after reading this book. That's a pretty big "hope" from a guy who feels totally unqualified to write even a short term paper, but the reason I can say such a thing with boldness is because I know God's purposes will be fulfilled for my life in writing this and in your life for reading it.

God loves to take the person who has lost hope that life could ever get any better and raise the bar for your dreams and aspirations beyond anything you could ever imagine. *I* am proof of that! My life has exceeded anything I ever imagined—and all because of God and for His glory. I pray that you will far surpass me, that you are the game changer who will move our world to the next level through the power of Jesus working in your life. Take your shot!